REGROWING
THE AMERICAN ECONOMY

The American Assembly, *Columbia University*

REGROWING
THE
AMERICAN ECONOMY

Prentice-Hall, Inc., *Englewood Cliffs, New Jersey*

A SPECTRUM BOOK

Library of Congress Cataloging in Publication Data
Main entry under title:

REGROWING THE AMERICAN ECONOMY

At head of title: The American Assembly, Columbia
University.
Edited by: G. W. Miller.
"A Spectrum Book."
Background papers prepared for the 63rd meeting of
the American Assembly at Arden House, Harriman, N.Y.,
Nov. 11-14, 1982.
Includes index.
I. United States—Economic policy—1981- —Con-
gresses. 2. International economic relations—Con-
gresses. I. Miller, G. William (George William) (date)
II. American Assembly.
HC106.8.R45 1983   338.973   83-3171
ISBN 0-13-771022-4
ISBN 0-13-771014-3 (pbk.)

Editorial/production supervision by Betty Neville
Cover design by Hal Siegel
Manufacturing buyer: Cathie Lenard

10 9 8 7 6 5 4 3 2 1

ISBN 0-13-771022-4

ISBN 0-13-771014-3 (PBK.)

PRENTICE-HALL INTERNATIONAL, INC. (*London*)
PRENTICE-HALL OF AUSTRALIA PTY. LIMITED (*Sydney*)
PRENTICE-HALL OF CANADA, INC. (*Toronto*)
PRENTICE-HALL OF INDIA PRIVATE LIMITED (*New Delhi*)
PRENTICE-HALL OF JAPAN, INC. (*Tokyo*)
PRENTICE-HALL OF SOUTHEAST ASIA PTE. LTD. (*Singapore*)
WHITEHALL BOOKS LIMITED (*Wellington, New Zealand*)
EDITORA PRENTICE-HALL DO BRASIL LTDA. (*Rio de Janeiro*)

Table of Contents

Preface

Much has been written in recent years lamenting the decline of the American economy from the position of preeminence which it enjoyed in the years immediately after World War II. These laments often fail to take into account two significant considerations. The first is that the earlier preeminence was artificially extraordinary and resulted in large measure from the destruction and disruption of the rest of the world's economy through the widespread ravages of the war. The second consideration is the fact that the United States, in the wake of the war, made a deliberate decision to help rebuild other economies so that the world would rest upon the cooperative interaction of a whole series of power centers rather than be divided into two ideological blocs in sharp confrontation.

Therefore, the ebullient existence of economies such as those of Japan and Western Europe, operating in strong competition with the United States, represents a triumphant success for the postwar policy of the United States and a signal achievement in the search for a more flexible world order. At the same time, the effectiveness of those economies, in competition with that of the United States, serves to provide timely warning to this country that changes are needed, not only in the way that its domestic economy is managed, but also in the way that an increasingly interdependent international system is organized.

Toward the end of 1982, when the United States and most of the world were in deep recession, there seemed a useful opportunity to examine the long-range economic policies that this country might pursue in order to assure its own balanced growth and to provide leadership to equitable, productive international recovery. Accordingly, The American Assembly convened a meeting among representatives of the Congress, the executive branch, business, organized labor, the universities, the legal profession, and the communications media at Arden House, Harriman, New York, from November 11 to 14, 1982. In preparation for that meeting, the Assembly commissioned the Honorable G. William Miller, former secretary of the Treasury, former chairman of the Federal Reserve Board, and former chairman of Textron, as editor and director of the undertaking. Under his editorial supervision, background papers on various aspects of the economy were prepared and read by the participants in the Arden House discussions, who produced a report recommending various policy changes.

Those background papers have been compiled into the present volume, which is published as a stimulus to further thinking and discussion about this subject among informed and concerned citizens. We hope this book will serve to provoke a broader national consensus for a program to restore the growth and vigor of our nation's economy and to improve the international economic system within which it operates.

Funding for this project was provided by the Alfred P. Sloan Foundation, the General Electric Foundation, The Continental Group, the Schalkenbach Foundation, Merrill Lynch, and Pfizer Inc. The opinions expressed in this volume are those of the individual authors and not necessarily those of the sponsors nor of The American Assembly, which does not take stands on the issues it presents for public discussion.

William H. Sullivan
President
The American Assembly

REGROWING
THE AMERICAN ECONOMY

G. *William Miller*

Introduction

During the summer of 1982, tremors ran through financial markets. Earlier the Drysdale and Penn Square failures had reverberated within the financial system. Mexico's debt and currency difficulties brought heightened concern. The possibility of a world banking crisis was openly discussed.

Was a financial crisis imminent? Would it trigger a global economic collapse? Was the American economy on the edge of a second Great Depression?

In August the New York markets suddenly exploded. A perception of relaxing monetary policy unleashed a major rally in both bond and stock prices. Trading volumes soared. Interest rates dropped sharply. The possibility of a major bull market as a prelude to strong economic recovery was openly touted.

Was the end of the recession at hand? Would it usher in a period of rapid economic growth world-wide? Was the American economy on the edge of a Great Expansion?

In truth, the underlying fundamentals did not support a short-term outlook for either collapse or boom. The greater cause for concern was and is the prospect for continuing stagnation.

G. WILLIAM MILLER *is a former secretary of the Treasury and a former chairman of the Federal Reserve Board. Before joining government service, he was chairman and chief executive officer of Textron Inc. He has served as a member of the National Foundation for the Humanities, chairman of The Conference Board, the U.S. Coast Guard Academy Foundation, the President's Committee for HIRE, and other national service organizations. Mr. Miller currently heads his own international merchant banking firm based in Washington, D.C.*

Challenge and Response

The purpose of this volume is to examine major challenges that the American economy will face in the coming years. To do so, it draws on the knowledge and experience of a wide spectrum of leading experts. They explore some of the policy alternatives for meeting those challenges successfully.

There is no attempt to be exhaustive. For example, the subject of energy is not directly addressed here. There also is no effort to forge a comprehensive program. Rather, the intention is to focus greater attention on key issues and to stimulate widespread discussions that can contribute to the formulation of America's responses.

That process began in November 1982 when fifty-nine men and women met at Arden House in Harriman, New York, for the Sixty-third American Assembly to discuss the topics covered in this volume. They came from Congress, the executive branch, business, organized labor, the law, the universities, and the communications media. At the end of three days, they reviewed a statement that represented general agreement on some of the main points that had been discussed during group sessions.

This introduction does not undertake to summarize the American Assembly statement or the material presented in the following chapters. Instead, it endeavors to reflect the general tone and direction that emerged at Arden House, and to set the stage for consideration of the more detailed expositions that follow.

The Need for Change

The American economy turned in a disappointing performance during the decade of the 1970s. Over the past ten to fifteen years, the United States economy has been characterized by slower real growth, higher unemployment, lower productivity, higher inflation, larger federal deficits, more volatility in economic and financial activities, growing difficulties in international trade and finance, and a series of structural problems relating to capital formation, productivity, technology, and resource utilization.

In the early 1980s the American economy has experienced one

of its most serious and painful recessions. The pattern has been much the same world-wide. Moreover, normal cyclical behavior seemed suspended. Economists have not been able to predict the timing and strength of recovery.

Nagging questions persist. Is the decline of the American economy only relative, in keeping with world cyclical conditions? Or has the United States lost its vitality and competitiveness? Is the American economy in eclipse, with a permanent fall from preeminence?

There can be no doubt but that the American economy has remarkable self-healing powers. Yet, these powers will not be sufficient to restore the American economy to its leading position. The depth and breadth and length of recession, the rise in inward-looking national policies and trade confrontations, the trend toward divergent and divisive actions among industrialized countries and between industrialized and developing countries, the strains on the international financial system, the growing importance of technologies, the rapid obsolescence of industrial facilities, the availability and price of energy and essential materials —all these and more are evidence that new approaches will be needed.

In order to assure an American economy second to none, adjustments will need to be made in economic policies and management to deal effectively with the new circumstances and to anticipate future changes. These changes will be pervasive and will certainly encompass relations between the United States and the world, between the public sector and the private sector, and between labor and management.

The renaissance of the American economy depends not upon waiting passively, but upon what America and Americans do to meet the challenge of change.

American Economic Goals

American policy should seek a dynamic, growing economy, capable of providing useful and satisfying work for all employable Americans, in an environment of reasonable price stability and equitable distribution of opportunity.

The immediate and overriding imperative is for vigorous and

sustained real economic growth. Only then will it be possible to attain long-term economic and social goals.

The benefits to Americans are many and compelling: more jobs and greater utilization of human resources, higher productivity to counter inflation, expanded investment and modernization, improved international competitiveness, lower federal deficits from both reduced outlays and higher revenues, conditions more conducive to lower real interest rates, sounder financing for Social Security, improved infrastructure, greater resources available for research and development, enhanced capacity to finance national defense, and higher standards of living.

A growing American economy is also a precondition for a prosperous world economy. A prosperous world economy is essential for stability and peace.

Realization of the benefits that flow from economic growth will help preserve individual liberties and contribute to general well-being.

Failure to restore economic growth entails social, political, and security risks for the entire world.

Short-term Policies for Growth

A new period of vigorous growth must begin with sustained recovery from recession. By traditional theory, built-in contra-cyclical mechanisms and specific fiscal actions to stimulate demand should assure recovery. In the meantime, lower money demand during recession should produce ample potential credit at lower interest rates and help fuel expansion. The size of the federal deficit during recession is one measure of the fiscal stimulus being applied.

The 1981–82 recession departed from the script. Fiscal policy, led by large tax cuts, moved into what seemed to be a highly stimulative posture. Deficits skyrocketed to record levels. Yet the expected stimulative effects did not materialize. The predicted recovery was delayed, uncertain, and potentially weak. At the same time, monetary policy, which had been mobilized to fight inflation, contributed to continued high real interest rates. Easy fiscal policy and tight monetary policy worked at cross purposes, so that economic recovery was illusive.

Among the factors that have retarded recovery and renewed growth are high interest rates which discouraged individuals and businesses from purchases and investments, high unemployment which reduced incomes and had a chilling effect on those who were working, declining world trade which is an increasingly important factor in the American economy, high debt burdens—public and private, domestic and international debt to finance continuing activities as well as new projects, and international monetary instability which added uncertainty to world trade and finance and investment.

Under these circumstances policy choices for growth are limited.

To do nothing would be to accept slow growth or stagnation.

To use fiscal policy for further stimulus would be unsound and counterproductive. In the absence of budgetary changes, record federal deficits are projected for years to come. These deficits would persist even with high employment, and thus represent a structural deficiency which needs correction not augmentation. Policies of increased spending or reduced revenues to stimulate the economy would further increase the structural deficits and adversely affect financial markets and inflationary expectations. The desired growth objectives would be frustrated.

To use monetary policy in isolation as the means for stimulating growth is also unwise. This would rekindle concerns about inflation, lead to higher interest rates, and choke off recovery.

The workable alternative is to stimulate real growth through a major change in the fiscal-monetary policy mix. This will require close coordination as to timing and balance.

The first key is a national commitment to reduce federal deficits. This would need to be accomplished over a reasonable time so as not to add to recessionary pressures. The President and the Congress should jointly adopt a program with specific targets for a progressive and significant reduction in the high employment deficit over a reasonable number of years. The program should accept the principle that both reductions in expenditures and increase in revenues are appropriate means of achieving the essential fiscal discipline.

With this commitment, monetary policy could then be directed toward generating more rapid economic growth without risking a significant acceleration of inflation. This can be done because of large amounts of unused production capacity, high unemployment, and ample supplies of food, fuels, and other raw materials.

The altered mix of fiscal and monetary policies should result in real interest rates more in line with historical experience.

Long-term Policies

As already noted, renewed economic growth is a precondition for solving underlying economic and social problems. Only then will it be possible to deal effectively with structural imperfections. Among these are high employment deficits, inadequate savings and productive investment, low productivity, mismatch of skills and jobs, and lack of international competitiveness in many product areas.

In order to make progress toward long-term economic goals, it is necessary to assure the proper overall environment. Sound macroeconomic policies—fiscal and monetary—must first be established and maintained. Beyond that, microeconomic policies are needed to deal with limited aspects of a diverse and changing economic system.

Macroeconomic policies have trended toward a divergence between the fiscal and monetary components. In industrial democracies, including the United States, parliaments (the President and the Congress under the American system) are constantly pressed by their constituents with demands for more expenditures and less taxes. As democracies mature, the spending obligations on behalf of special groups tend to accumulate, adding layer upon layer. It has proven easier for parliaments to accept increased deficit financing than to make the hard choices between spending less or taxing more. As deficits become a permanent way of life and relentlessly expand, governments place more and more burdens on their central banks to offset the easy fiscal stance and restrain inflation through restrictive monetary policies.

The resulting fiscal-monetary mix contributes to poor economic performance.

Likewise, many microeconomic policies have been developed in response to the perceived needs of special constituencies. This has not always resulted in efficient or effective programs or given adequate regard to the general public interest.

Long-term economic policies must therefore be directed toward maintaining an improved fiscal-monetary mix growing out of shorter-term actions to impose greater fiscal discipline and concentrating microeconomic policies on developing human resources, enhancing technological capabilities, facilitating orderly adjustments for impacted industries, and moderating hardships for people and communities affected by economic change.

Fiscal Policy

Fiscal policy should be retained as a major instrument of economic management. It has an important role to play as a contracyclical stabilizer. The ideal fiscal posture is one which produces a neutral influence—that is, a balanced budget—in times of high employment. In times of recession, deficits provide needed stimulus for recovery. In periods of boom, surpluses restrain over-expansion and thus help to retard inflation.

There has been some inconsistency in the administration's view of fiscal stance. On the one hand, it has been suggested that the huge deficits are tolerable because they represent a smaller percentage of gross national product than deficits in countries like Japan and West Germany. But those countries have national savings rates much higher in relation to GNP than the United States, so that even after the "negative" savings represented by deficits, they have a larger net savings pool than in America. As a consequence, the share of aggregate credit absorbed by the government is much higher in the U.S.

On the other hand, the administration supports a so-called "balanced budget" amendment to the Constitution. This support is apparently founded on the proposition that big deficits are bad for America's economic health.

A constitutional amendment to mandate a "balanced budget" implies a rigid requirement. This would remove fiscal policy as an effective policy instrument. Actually, the proposed amendment would not outlaw deficits, but instead require a congressional supermajority to authorize a deficit. This has drawbacks. It could lead to stalemate, with no supermajority for a deficit and no simple majority for a balanced budget. Or it could lead to greater use of off-budget techniques to accomplish desired ends.

The solution lies not in a constitutional change, but in the political will—perhaps encouraged by the growing political restraint of the ballot box—to restore fiscal discipline.

That political will should be supported with effective budget procedures. The federal budget process has been improved over the past decade, but further strengthening is desirable. One important step would be to include off-budget expenditures in the budget. There should also be improved presentation within the budget of capital expenditures, trust fund budgets, and tax expenditures. Federal credit operations, trust funds, and tax expenditures should receive full congressional review during each budget cycle.

The ultimate objective, of course, is not process but results. In order to reduce the projected large structural deficits sufficiently, it will be necessary to consider both reductions in spending and increases in revenues. As already indicated, these should be targeted over a reasonable number of years so as not to impede recovery from the serious 1981–82 recession.

EXPENDITURES

The opportunities for spending cuts are somewhat limited. After recent curtailments, a very large percentage of federal outlays are not comprised of defense, non-need related entitlements, and interest on the national debt. The magnitude of deficit reduction needed will not be achieved unless the rate of growth is slowed in the areas of defense spending and entitlements.

REVENUES

The revenue side must not be overlooked. As the rate of increase in spending slows and the targets for further cuts are limited more and more to programs which are socially justified and needed or politically immune, then the only alternative for sound fiscal policy is to raise sufficient revenues.

In searching for equitable ways to increase revenues, consideration should be given to broader resort to user fees. This follows the principle of linking benefits with costs. Tax simplification would also be desirable.

The individual federal income tax system should be simplified by greatly limiting the allowable deductions and credits. This would permit lower general rates.

A shift of the tax burden toward consumption and away from savings and investment would be beneficial in helping to correct some structural problems. This might be accomplished within the present income tax system by allowing larger exclusions from income for net savings by individuals. Some integration of corporate income taxes with the personal income tax would also be helpful.

In any case, the principle of progressivity—recognizing ability to pay—should be retained.

One important way to increase revenues is to collect the taxes that are already due. The revenues lost from noncompliance have grown at an alarming rate. Greater resources should be devoted to assuring full collection of taxes and other debts due to the federal government. Every effort should be made to reinforce the fundamental policy of voluntary assessment and compliance.

Monetary Policy

Monetary policy in the U.S. has evolved during this century in response to major changes in the American financial and economic systems. The Federal Reserve came into being in 1913 after a series of money panics had rocked the nation. The immediate purposes contemplated by the founders for the new Federal Reserve System were to provide greater flexibility in the flow of money and credit, enhance liquidity for banks, and improve supervision of banking. The broader objective was, and remains, to help in realizing the nation's goals of economic growth, employment, and price stability.

The American monetary system has continued to evolve over the years, reflecting changes in both the domestic and international economies. The Federal Reserve has been changed both by legislation and in practice to accommodate to altered circumstances. In the post-Depression era, the Federal Reserve gained an increased measure of independence within the government.

In the years after World War II, monetary controls exercised by the Federal Reserve were augmented by built-in limits on the growth of credit. In particular, the interest rate ceilings on savings accounts and various usury laws tended themselves to limit credit flows during expansion.

More recently, there have been extensive financial innovations fostered by inflationary pressures, international conditions, and technological advances. Inventions of new financial accounts and instruments, and the growing ability of nondepositary institutions to provide a wide range of financial services to individuals and businesses, effectively undermined the restraints imposed by interest rate ceilings. For example, the introduction of repurchase agreements and NOW accounts reintroduced the payment of interest on checking accounts, and the advent of money market mutual funds hastened the decline of interest-limited savings accounts.

These and other developments created a rapid expansion in financial devices that represent "near money" and financial institutions that represent "near banks." The task of the Federal Reserve became increasingly difficult.

In the last few years, a great deal of debate about monetary policy has focused on Federal Reserve operating procedures. The Federal Reserve's shift in October 1979 to emphasis on bank reserves in controlling the rate of growth of narrow monetary aggregates has been given great attention. Whatever the technique, the real policy question is what is it that the Federal Reserve should control.

The specific aggregates targeted by the Federal Reserve should not be so narrow as to have a weak connection to the broad objectives of economic policy nor so broad as to be only minimally affected by the policy instruments under its control. The Federal Reserve recognized this in late 1982 when it temporarily abandoned the use of M-1, which was being affected by rapid changes in financial instruments.

The Federal Reserve should give greater emphasis to factors other than the narrower monetary aggregates in establishing its targets and objectives.

The independence of the Federal Reserve within the government should be preserved. This places a responsibility on the Federal Reserve, the administration, and the Congress to address and to reconcile any inconsistencies in their economic goals and projections.

Summary

For more than a decade, economic performance has been disappointing—in all directions of the compass. The American economy has itself shown evidence of decline, both in cyclical weakness and in longer-term symptoms of structural deficiencies affecting vitality and international competitiveness.

Despite the powerful forces of change at work in the world, there is no inherent reason why the American economy should not rise out of these difficulties and reconfirm its position of economic preeminence. The American private enterprise system is fundamentally sound, with remarkable capacity for self-correction. This natural tendency toward self-healing could be reinforced by improved cooperation between the public and private sectors, between labor and management, and between the United States and both the developed and developing countries.

Above all, the rise of the American economy depends upon government policies which meet the challenges of change in establishing and maintaining a climate conducive to balanced growth, high employment, and price stability. The following chapters explore many of the options and suggest specific policy directions that could contribute to a new era of progress for the American economy.

Albert T. Sommers

1

The Evolution of Economic Policy:

Preparing for Long-Term Recovery

In surveying the challenges confronting the United States economy over the next decade, this chapter shamelessly raises large issues for which it has only partial answers, or no answers at all. Its perspective is historical and institutional, not that of formal economics. It seeks to describe how the American economy has arrived at its present institutional predicaments and what kinds of changes may be required to move toward a more effective integration of institutions.

The chapter's evolutionary viewpoint accepts the mixed economy, with all its frustrations, as an unavailable reality of the present and of the future. It argues that growth is the imperative for a mixed economy; without it, the mixture is unstable. To achieve growth in the 1980s, we need adjustments in both fiscal and monetary equipment; we need to develop an American version of an "industrial policy" to stimulate growth of fixed capital;

ALBERT T. SOMMERS *is a senior vice president and chief economist for The Conference Board. He is a fellow of the National Association of Business Economists and a member of several economic and business associations. In addition to serving as director of several organizations and an economic adviser to the Ford Foundation, Mr. Sommers has also written numerous articles on various economic issues.*

we need a substantial effort at improving human resources. These changes are required to reconcile a vigorous, growing private economy with the continuing growth of public purposes that is implicit in democracy and technology.

Formal Economics and Social Evolution

Formal economics deals with economic consequences as exclusively a function of economic causality; it views economic performance as a reflection of the degrees of adherence to, and departure from, a set of eternal laws (drawn from summations of individual self-interest) which governs normal and healthy economic performance. Such normative systems need not entirely ignore historical changes in social, political, technological, and other institutional conditions, but they tend to treat these conditions as incidental, or as economics-determining.

Formal economics is disinclined to treat economic history as transpiring in an evolving context whose evolutionary principles come largely from outside economics. The "equilibrium" of equilibrium economics applies only within the economic system itself; it does not address the relationship between the economic system and the changing political, social, and technological context in which economic activity transpires. Indeed, mathematical treatment of economic evidence is profoundly timeless and nonevolutionary; the structural equations of theoretical economics require long periods of data—the larger the number of variables, the longer the required data base—to achieve statistical respectability. But in an evolving historical and institutional context, the current value of past data requires a progressive discount for age as the system they purport to describe changes through time.

The U.S. economy has evolved into the 1980s. Closed mathematical systems do not undergo transition. Now, as always, the U.S. economic system is in transition, and not simply a transition from Keynesian economics to monetarism and supply-side economics, although it is partly in that transition also. It is in transition now because history has been exerting evolutionary pressure for change on parts of an institutional structure that seemed to work well for the first thirty years of the postwar period.

Reaganomics itself is much more than its monetarist and supply-side principles; its anticipated return to smaller government, balanced budgets, free markets, and heightened individual incentive is rooted in a philosophy. The philosophy is very attractive to economists (including this one), partly because it implies an increase in the economist's power to analyze and conclude. But life was not designed to please economists. It is not clear how widely the philosophy is shared among older citizens who recall economic conditions before the postwar prosperity, or among younger citizens who have spent their entire working lives in the presence of a growing and activist government that has sought to reduce economic risk, to soften the penalty for individual failure, and to control the effects of technology. Whether or not government has been "right" to undertake these things, it has done them because it had to do them—for political, social, and technological reasons. And in doing them it has produced durable attitudes, expectations, and institutions that are unlikely to disappear.

However much it has changed the players, Reaganomics has not importantly changed the institutions it inherited, and it is philosophically opposed to the creation of new institutions. The dilemma confronting the Reagan administration in the early 1980s is that it is prepared to challenge a set of institutions and attitudes that were part of the postwar consensus, but it has no clear mandate to revert to an earlier set—to evolve backwards—and the course forward is, as always, uncharted and fraught with political risk and economic uncertainty. An inevitable starting point in exploring this institutional dilemma is the institutional history itself. Precisely because economic history describes an evolving system, a seamless web, it is not easy to pick a starting point, but beginning with conditions at the end of World War II should suffice to make some necessary observations.

The Postwar Institutional Structure

In 1946, a great dawn broke over the U.S. economy. For seventeen years the system had lived through, first, the most violently depressed decade in its history, and then six years of war so nearly total that in its final phase over 40 percent of all output was dedicated to it. Depression and war starved both consumption and investment in the private sector. But technology had accumulated in the absence of private markets for its exploitation, and the nominal liquidity of the system had been violently increased by wartime multiplication of financial assets, while the levels of wages and prices had been constrained by a powerful system of direct controls. Demands had been deferred; technological commercialization had been deferred; levels of debt had been shrunk; real liquidity had been multiplied; a generation had been held off the market by war. From mid–1945 to mid–1947, 12 million highly energized young Americans, off to a late start in building their own version of the American way of life, fanned out into the labor market and into the depleted markets for homes and consumer goods, precipitating one of the great ages of growth, investment, and advance in living standards experienced by any economy at any time.

These immense energies were conditioned by a set of ethical resolutions that had taken shape in the institutional change precipitated by the experience of the 1930s. As the business system began reconversion from its wartime composition in early 1946, the first postwar Congress put in place another ethically oriented cornerstone; a commitment of government to achieve a broadly distributed prosperity for all. The cornerstone was to be built upon very heavily.

At the end of World War II, the U.S. enjoyed an unprecedented dominance militarily, technologically, and in terms of living standards. Equipped with the only hard currency in the world, and the only surviving advanced industrial base, it shouldered its developing ethical commitments easily, with no visible strain. The postwar ethic was not a necessary condition for the achievement of the widespread prosperity of the first postwar decade, which was assured in any event by the release of an immense tide of effective demand. In turn, conditions in the first postwar decade were so generally prosperous that the programs were hardly necessary and remained underdeveloped, particularly in contrast to their earlier and more rapid development in Europe. In the eyes of that large part of the work force that remembered the Depression very well, the commitment to sustained prosperity may not even have been a *credible* commitment, in the sense that it was not at all clear that government was capable of living up to the full-employment determination expressed in the legislation. Even in the 1930s, rapid innovations by government had hardly produced dramatic results.

In the early 1960s, the economic energy provided by depression and war was beginning to falter, technologically competitive economies were beginning to make their appearance in Europe and Asia, and the national sense of technological supremacy was fractured by "sputnik." The so-called "new economics"—a highly successful practical application of a modest (and not new) insight into fiscal policy—restored the energy, but it did more than that. Its widely recognized success has two profound consequences.

In the first instance it seemed to demonstrate the power of governmental economic policy to fulfill its obligations under the commitment to high employment. Thereafter, any substantial shortfall from general prosperity would be viewed not as an act of God, or as an unavoidable encounter with the mysteries of the business cycle, but as a failure of government—either intentional and conspiratorial or stupid. A second consequence was that the prosperity of the middle 1960s—unaccompanied by any indications of inflation or other costs that could be associated with highly stimulative policy—suggested a reserve of power in collective action sufficient to go after the remaining disparities, "injustices," and "inequities" in the system—inequities that appeared both more visible and more unnecessary by contrast with the general prosperity in which they were imbedded.

THE FIRST WATERSHED: FROM AGGREGATIVE TO
DISTRIBUTIVE POLICIES

In the decade beginning with 1965, and in the face of an unpopular and unfinanced war, the United States, having achieved virtually full employment of its enormous resources and confident of its ability to grow, multiplied its social objectives as never before. In that decade, the system extended its economic commitment far beyond high employment itself; it elevated and broadened its goals to assure not just jobs for all, but security for all, a major equalization of incomes, equality of opportunity, extended education for all, improved health, reconstruction of the environment, improvement of the cities, rebuilding of the housing stock —in a word, to reach distributive justice at home and full participation for all in American abundance. Politics joined with demonstrated power to raise the role of government another big notch.

In less ambitious times, the insatiable demand in this economic system, as in all systems, was conventional consumption; the free market, equipped with only the most general fiscal and monetary equipment, could be expected to frustrate these demands with reasonable efficiency (and considerable cyclical fluctuation) and contain the effective demand within the available resources. Starting in 1965, the system faced multiple instabilities while its power to contain them within the available resources was held within quite conventional limits. Accepted goals simply raced ahead of accepted means; the resulting inflation was fought (and is still being fought) not by deliberate allocation or arraying of priorities or by "planning," but by the conventional aggregative equipment inherited from earlier, less ambitious decades. Inevitably, the aggregative equipment began to reach confrontation after confrontation with the inflation implicit in the multiple goals, and the intensity of the business cycle, which had been waning in the decade from 1955 to 1965, began to increase. Two attempts (in 1971–1974 and 1978–1980) to supplement aggregative economic policy with a "social contract" to restrain inflation ended in apparent failure. (A generally similar attempt in the early 1960s may or may not have been "successful," but it did seem to enlist a higher degree of cooperation.)

The year 1965 can be described as a genuine watershed—not because of the growth of the Vietnam War, but because of the shift of governmental objectives from targets of aggregative growth to essentially distributive targets. Within an unchanged policy context, public programs and publicly assumed responsibilities grew rapidly in numbers and in budgetary costs. Transfer payments rose from about 25 percent of all budget outlays in 1965 to over 40 percent in 1975. Social welfare expenditures advanced from about 7 percent of the gross national product (GNP) in the early postwar years to 11 percent in the first half of the 1960s; by 1976, they had climbed to over 19 percent of GNP.

THE SECOND WATERSHED: THE END OF GROWTH IN
LIVING STANDARDS

This is not the place to review the programs involved in this assault on distributive inequality. Some of the programs have been generally classed as successful, some as unsuccessful, some partly successful but inefficient, and some of them were swamped by abuse. But by late in the 1970s, the postwar consensus that had unanimously supported the first round of postwar social programs and gave generous support to the second round beginning in 1965 began to waver and then to break up.

There were doubtless many reasons for the loss of faith in government's response to social problems and the loss of political support for the costs. Among these, and perhaps predominant, was the end of growth in real output and the beginning of an actual decline in real living standards. Inflation was widely believed to be responsible for the decline in living standards. This conclusion is unsupported by economics since income inflation is an inevitable accompaniment of indigenous domestic inflation; but aggregative, undifferentiated monetary assaults on inflation (much of which was imported energy inflation) induced progressively severe short-term recessions, carrying long-term costs in immense cyclicity, deferral of investment, and retarded productivity.

The arresting of growth of living standards, and then its decline, were consequences, first of all, of the end of secular growth in productivity. The inevitable arresting of living standards from this cause was intensified by international invasions of the American living standard—by OPEC, on the one hand, and by the increasing grip on domestic and third markets held by Japan and, to a lesser degree, West Germany. A third element in the subsidence of real growth, and part of the explanation of the national productivity performance, was an enormous growth in the labor force—a demographic echo of the birth rates following the end of World War II—combined with a sociologically rooted uptrend in the percentage of women in the labor force. Both of these conditions urged economic policy in the direction of stimulus, and the resulting aggregate growth in employment was the highest in the developed world. But the average maturity, experience, and training of the labor force doubtless suffered in the absorption process. Finally, the composition of jobs continued its postwar shift away from goods industries—where productivity gain is easily achieved and easily measured—to service occupations—where neither achievement nor measurement is easy. (The rise in the rate of female participation in the labor force will surely flatten out, and the demographics of labor force growth will reverse in a few years; the relative growth of services is increasingly a function of weak performance of goods industries, traceable in part to goods imports.)

If the shift from aggregative to distributive objectives of policy in 1965 marked one watershed in the postwar years, the end of growth in real living standards around the middle of the 1970s marked another. The political and policy experience since 1975— the identification of inflation as public enemy number one and the subordination of job goals to inflation goals—attests to an alteration of the impact of distributive policies. Once the growth in living standards subsided, further progress in the distributive goals could no longer be achieved simply by differential distribution of an *increment* of output; increasingly, the costs of the redistribution came to require a taking away of resources from some in order to give to others. Inflation and "bracket creep" elevated marginal tax rates affecting middle-income Americans and raised tax receipts, but inflation itself enlarged the costs of the transfer programs and seemed to rule out tax rate relief.

POLITICAL AND SOCIAL PROBLEMS REMAIN

The apparent political unwillingness of the system to support the redistributive goals pursued so intensively in the decade beginning in 1965 nevertheless leaves substantial political and social problems in place. The programs of that decade are difficult to unwind, as the Reagan administration would ruefully agree, and the failure of many of them has left the problems to which they were directed still unresolved. Moreover, the reversal of attitudes toward these programs does not appear to be at all complete or enduring; poll after poll reveals a public unwillingness to abandon specific programs, even in the presence of dissatisfaction with the aggregate costs.

Virtually all of the working population of the United States has lived its entire life in a mixed economy, with its perplexing mixture of individual freedom and aggregative social objectives. There remain all of the problems posed by the immensely different distribution of political and economic power that are the hallmark of democratic free-market systems. The interdependence that is an inevitable consequence of technological development continues to intensify, and the "externalities" of technology—in the environment and in the workplace—continue to evoke support for government regulation. The unquestioned efficiencies of private markets still fail to serve all of the public purposes to which modern mixed economies inevitably dedicate themselves. Technology increasingly calls for the development of intensive skills and training in the labor force as the definition of investment moves away from heavy outlay on traditional plant and equipment and toward the incorporation of advanced knowledge, education, and technical skills. The treatment of labor input continues to be distinguished progressively from the treatment of all other inputs; the presumed "right" to a job still conflicts with the free-market "right" of the owners of capital to invest and disinvest for economic reasons alone.

These ethical quandaries of the democratic mixed economy are absolutely inherent in its structure. Whether this is desirable or not in any ultimate sense, or whether it is or is not convenient for economic theory, there is no historical escape from them. Democracy and technology are responsible for the growth of public purpose. The market system serves private purposes efficiently but serves public purposes only by accident, and its public impact is often perverse. The ethical component of the mixed economy, inevitably conducted by government, serves public purposes, but inefficiently. In the course of its pursuit of public purposes, it often impairs the efficiency of markets. Modern democratic societies are equipped not only with efficient means, which do not seek all the desired ends, but also with desired ends, for which the available means are inherently inefficient. (Government often inherits responsibilities just because there is no economically efficient private way of executing them.) The imposition of ethical content on a market system involves inefficient means, absorbs resources for purposes not reflected in conventional measures of output, and reduces the efficiency of markets; this is the ultimate source of inflation in modern Western societies. It underlies, is precedent to, and is upstream from the monetary and fiscal developments which economists identify as the proximate cause of inflation. The application of restrictive fiscal and monetary policies can divert the influence of those historical conditions from inflation to the real world of output and employment, but only temporarily; it cannot change the history or the institutional trend.

The Growth Imperative

The challenge posed to the American economy in the next decade is simply that the reconciliation of market mechanisms and public purposes is achievable in the presence of vigorous economic growth; it is unachievable, and even dangerous, if growth falters or reverses. Paradoxically, the political and ethical evolution of the mixed economy demands growth at the same time that it tends to inhibit it. In the 1980s, the imperative for the United States is to grow, and to grow without abandoning the public purposes to which it is inevitably committed by democracy, technology, and humanism. It cannot escape its ethical content, but it can no longer afford the "soft" ethic it managed so easily in the first twenty-five years of the postwar period. It needs a "hard" ethic that limits the impact of social programs on growth, and it needs the tools to guide a more complex system toward growth.

The same problem confronts all Western democracies; all of them have sought conservative policies to arrest inflation, and all of them will henceforth be seeking policies to stimulate growth. Policy devices that arrest inflation at the expense of growth are temporary expedients and dangerous if prolonged. The aggregative fiscal and monetary policies inherited from an earlier era when economics was uncomplicated by the progressive evolution of the mixed economy cannot alone assure vigorous growth, low inflation, and the equalitarian trend required by democratic mixed economies. Those economies that break with tradition and develop the institutions to meet these complex demands will fare better than others—indeed, their better performance will be at the expense of others. The U.S. performance in the decade depends upon a hard reexamination of our policy equipment and a willingness to modernize policy equipment where required. Reaganomics represents a warranted correction of practice; its failures thus far —the unemployment, the falling rate of private investment, the excessively high interest rates—seem to call for evolution in the equipment it allows itself.

The Dilemma of Fiscal and Monetary Policy

In the United States, and all throughout the West, fiscal and monetary policies have turned in the direction of fighting inflation, and all over the West these policies have enjoyed a Pyrrhic victory. The inflation rate has declined in varying degrees among countries, but almost all of them have experienced the serious side effects of antiinflationary policy; throughout both Europe and North America, unemployment rates are flirting with postwar records. The economic suppression attributable, at least in part, to suppressive monetary policy has inevitably suppressed the revenue base in virtually all of these countries and added to debt service requirements; as a result, virtually all of them are experiencing large deficits in their fiscal accounts. In turn, the deficits augment the problems confronted by monetary policy and thus tend to aggravate the interest rate conditions that contribute to the deficit. The runaway deficit dimensions that are in prospect in the United States are partly a function of this circular relationship between conservative monetary policy and fiscal outcomes. (They also reflect a growing defense burden on the budget and the regrettably large tax reduction bill legislated in 1981.)

These conditions, prevalent throughout the West, are the consequence of a monetary assault on inflation that cannot be validated by a fiscal assault; that is, the democratic mixed economies throughout the West are simply not in an evolutionary position to substantially reduce their percentage of outlays directed toward social and redistributive objectives. The shrinkage of credit availability thus falls heavily on the private sector. The interest rates that result from conservative monetary policy in the presence of fiscal positions highly resistant to spending reductions elevate nominal interest rates, magnify recession, and then produce spectacular real interest rates as the inflation rate subsides in the course of recession. This is, roughly, the present position of the United States, replicated, with circumstantial differences, almost throughout the societies whose history resembles our own.

The circularity between the application of restrictive monetary policy and fiscal deficits goes beyond just the effects on the revenue base, and on debt service. The interest rates that inevitably result from this process have their heaviest impact on private investment, and, because of the consequences for investment and productivity, the trend of *potential* output is suppressed far into the future. If the great imperative for mixed economies in the 1980s is to achieve vigorous growth, the combination of policies in place today simply does not serve the imperative.

THE POLICIES THEMSELVES

Apart from the unfortunate interactions of fiscal and monetary policy, each branch of policy has deep and pervasive problems of its own. At least in the United States, neither set of policies has participated in or reflected the institutional evolution that has so altered the economy to which the policies are directed.

The interpretation of budgetary outcomes in the United States is now in a state of incoherence. The prevailing orthodoxy calls for a balanced federal budget, as a sustainable and desirable long-run condition; but the budget has not been balanced in a decade, and deficits averaging $200 billion a year overhang the system for the next three years. The moralistic position that the federal government, like a family, should balance its income and outgo has been honored in the breach in twenty-four of the past thirty years. Every administration in the postwar years has promised a balanced budget and even forecast a balanced budget several years out; the balance evaporates as we approach it. Thirty years ago, when the private sector was still enjoying its postwar vigor, when private debt was still very low and rising, and when federal government expenditures were very largely for highly stimulative direct purchases, it would have been nearly impossible to run a budget deficit if we tried; now it appears to be impossible to avoid one.

Influenced by monetarists, some of whom argue that budget deficits themselves have no bearing on inflation, and by supply-siders, some of whom place tax reduction far above budget outcomes in their own priorities, even conservative economists within the Reagan administration have argued that deficits are unimportant or tolerable as a "necessary evil."

Improvements have been made in the organization of the budget and in the legislative process of budgeting. But the federal budget itself remains a paradoxical and misleading document. In its present form, it is nothing more than a federal cash flow; on the same accounting, American Telephone & Telegraph would report annual deficits of $5 billion. It lacks consolidated financial statements that would properly treat acquisitions and sales of assets, and it runs no capital account, making no separation of long-term acquisitions from consumables and services. Budget outcomes in the United States have been warped by the conflicting pressures of rapidly growing social programs on the one hand and lip service dedication to a literally balanced budget on the other. As a consequence, spending on the U.S. infrastructure of public facilities has been shrunk to a smaller and smaller share of total outlays.

The separation of the federal budget into a current account and a capital account would be a response to some of these problems. Balancing the current account would present some of the same difficulties that confront the application of a balanced budget constitutional requirement, since the current account will reflect the ebb and flow of revenues induced by the business cycle, but it would be possible to balance it over the cycle with a fluctuating operating reserve. It is also true that the definition of a capital item for the federal government is more complicated than its definition for purposes of a private enterprise; a continuously widening definition would run the risks of continuous growth in the financing requirements of government. But the potential advance—in restraining the growth of current outlays, in providing continuous funding of investment in infrastructure, and perhaps also in integrating the disorderly array of subsidies, tax expenditures, sales and debt incurrence of off-budget agencies and government-sponsored agencies—appears to be impressive, and the long record of net disinvestment in public facilities (and perhaps defense as well) argues for it.

Popular views of the federal debt and its growth raise a similar set of issues. We do not treat either personal or corporate debt in their absolute amounts; we sensibly relate them to the assets and income flows available for service of the debt. But the federal debt is still commonly treated as a dollar amount, without reference to growth of government assets, the growth of the income stream available for the servicing of the debt through taxation, and the growth of GNP itself. Aggregate federal debt declined, as a percentage of GNP, until only a few years ago. The relationship did not decline in 1981 because of emerging recession in the private sector. It rose in 1982 because of recession and tax reduction. And it threatens to rise in 1983–1985 because of defense accelerations and further tax reductions. But the postwar record is far from hopeless, despite rises in the dollar measure of the debt itself.

Some degree of growth in the public debt outstanding (not the temporarily violent growth that would lie ahead in the absence of any adjustment to the prospective budgets for fiscal years 1983 and beyond) now seems to be unavoidable, and even desirable. But the growth of the outstanding debt should and can be at a more stable *rate* than the wildly oscillating experience of the past dozen years. The debt incurrence should be related to, and should finance, the investment of government, not its expenses. In developed Western economies, the federal sector appears to require a call on the capital market for its own legitimate investment purposes, but not an endless call and not a violently fluctuating call. The objective should be acceptance of public debt formation, effective control over its rate, and an accounting relationship between debt formation and public investment.

The equipment available to monetary policy also would benefit from a reexamination, leading to an enlargement and refinement of its powers. As it is now conducted, and in the presence of violent swings in the Department of Treasury financing requirements, monetary policy in the United States is producing painfully volatile interest rates whose consequences are reflected in volatile general economic experience. All of the recessions of the past fifteen years have followed upon a critical scarcity of funds accompanied by soaring rates, and the impact of the rates has fallen heavily on investment. The Federal Reserve System inevitably exercises a disciplinary responsibility for controlling inflation.

But its equipment for the purpose has remained highly general and nonselective. The Federal Reserve System is equipped only to conduct a nuclear war against inflation; it has typically failed to make use of selective controls over credit or other innovative, nonprice restraints on credit. For much of the postwar years, and most dramatically during the 1970s, innovations in financial markets have kept far ahead of the system's ability to maintain order; its preoccupation with its inflation responsibilities has often led it to ignore its responsibilities to meet the credit requirements of the economy.

The Federal Reserve System's shift toward a monetarist concern with money stock has not solved these problems, and in some respects it has magnified them. Monetarism assumes that its restrictive burden falls on output in the short term, while attitudes adjust to the prospect of lower inflation; thereafter, its restraint rests exclusively on inflation itself. This view is held by almost all central banks in the West, and it therefore sounds presumptuous to challenge it. But at this writing, virtually all of the West has been trapped into years of high unemployment, with its associated costs, and low investment, with its implications for productivity. At least in the U.S., inflation has been beaten down to what may be *too low* a rate—below the rate required by a developed mixed economy to absorb its social costs (as well as its fix-price and large service components). In a chapter on inflation for the 1980 American Assembly publication *The Economy and the President: 1980 and Beyond,* I suggested the term "natural rate of inflation" as a logical counterpart to the monetarist "natural rate of unemployment." In effect this suggests that there is a positive NAURI (non-accelerating–unemployment rate of inflation) as counterpart to the negative NAIRU (non-accelerating–inflation rate of unemployment). The evidence since 1980 seems to support this view, but the real test will come with recovery. This is not to say that inflation is "good"; but neither is unemployment "good," and the consequence of a frontal monetary assault on inflation in a mixed economy is a violent rise in unemployment. The mixed economy is a product of socioeconomic evolution; evolutionary processes do not present isolated "problems" detachable from their context and amenable to "solution" through manipulation of one or a few policy variables.

A response to inflation must thus be as broad as its causes, and it must take a realistic, not narrowly economic, view of its enemy. The reasons why governments have created "too much" money and run "too big" deficits are the ultimate reasons for inflation— the "final" causes, as distinguished from the "efficient" or "proximate" causes. Money creation and budget deficits are the visible, measurable economic causes of inflation; they leave a statistical trail leading forward to inflation that has been surveyed to almost everyone's satisfaction, and its study has doubtless produced some useful guides to monetary and fiscal policy. But the trail leading backward to the final causes of inflation has gotten much less attention than it deserves. The causes of both the money creation and the deficits are political, scientific, and ethical, rather than economic. They involve democratic institutions, the acceleration of technology, and a humanistic conception of what holds a society together. The interconnections between the inflation rate, on the one hand, and our social and technological history, on the other, do not lend themselves to the quantitative method of economics, but they are obvious enough. The ultimate causes of inflation are also the causes of substantial departures in our economic system from the steady-state, free-market assumptions that underlie economics generally and monetarism in particular. This leaves plenty of room for useful contributions on the part of economics, but those willing to accept a historical and evolutionary view of where this system is now are entitled to have their doubts about narrowly based antiinflationary policies and what their consequences are likely to be.

At least in some degree, the failure of U.S. investment over the last decade and the associated failure of productivity to grow along its long-term trend are traceable to anachronisms in our views of how a federal budget should perform in a modern social system and of the nature and responsibilities of the Federal Reserve System. To serve our purposes well in the 1980s, both sets of institutions could benefit from a conceptual realignment. If it should be acknowledged that budget deficits are not a defeat for policy and are in fact a necessary call on capital available for federal government financing of its investment, it would become possible to avoid the violent cyclical fluctuations in the deficit (and in economic behavior) that are progressively visible in the record of the last fifteen years. If the Federal Reserve System were to accept a wider range of powers, including variable restraints on the demand for credit aimed at speculation and consumption, it could contribute to the financing of such deficits with some inflation (the "natural rate"), but no long-term acceleration of inflation in a less cyclical environment that would foster private investment. The more stable behavior of the entire system (including interest rates) in such a structure, together with the higher rate of investment that would result from a stable environment for the planning of private investment, would yield efficiencies in many forms—more stable and productive employment conditions (thereby minimizing the inevitable friction between the "right" to a job and the "right" to hire and fire) and even a reduced growth rate of all the transfer systems that in one way or another reflect the high level and great variability of unemployment. Federal Reserve System financing of the moderate and stable federal deficits that would be the objective of such a system would not really *cause* inflation; instead, it would validate a rate of inflation that appears to be unavoidable in a modern social and technological context. It would therefore help to moderate the substantial and punishing cycles in activity, unemployment, interest rates, and investment rates that have been experienced in the past several years.

The Investment Rate in the 1980s

The U.S. economy offers its resident businesses the largest consumer market by far in the world and, in most respects, the largest base of natural resources to draw on in serving the market. A century of these prevailing conditions, accompanied by spectacular marketing effort, has produced the most consumption-oriented society in the West. The consumption orientation has actually grown over the last decade when the conditions on which it rested clearly deteriorated. Postmarket redistribution (see below) of purchasing power has contributed to this outcome by enhancing consumption and retarding output.

There are few economists in the country who would disagree with the proposition that in terms of its own long-term future the United States overconsumes and underinvests; and the opinion might be virtually unanimous if the rate of public investment (in infrastructure and in defense) were to be included on the investment side of the relationship. This opinion is so widespread that the very large personal tax reductions contained in the 1981 Tax Reduction Act had to take their political justification mainly from their uncertain effects on productivity and saving, rather than from their more dependable effects on consumption itself.

There is much that can be done to reshape this consumption-investment position, and there is even much agreement on how it ought to be done. The U.S. tax structure favors consumption by taxing income; it taxes income saved (and even the income from income saved) along with taxing income spent. It allows the most liberal deductions for interest costs of any developed economy. Our credit market institutions cater far more to consumption than in any other developed or undeveloped country. The consumption share of output in the United States is fully ten percentage points higher than in Germany and probably twenty percentage points higher than in Japan; consumer credit extension is higher than anywhere else, and it is more volatile cyclically. Until the revision of allowed depreciation in the 1981 tax act, the U.S. had by far the slowest recapture of the historical cost of investment; the new law is an improvement, but it still leaves recapture slower than in many other developed countries (the revenue losses from personal tax reduction have required cancellation of some of the improvement).

Changes in fiscal and monetary policy to contain the consumption share and enlarge the investment share are difficult politically, but they are essential to a revival of American growth. In all mixed economies, private investment is on the defensive. The readjustment of shares can be achieved only in the presence of vigorous business conditions; controlling extension of consumer credit through *generally* high interest rates that subdue investment along with consumption simply does not serve the purpose. If high general interest rates available to the saver stimulate real saving—and there is much controversy over the savings response to interest rates—they also depress employment and, hence, the very incomes from which the saving is intended to be drawn. Over the last year, in the presence of generally very high rewards to savers, some tax reduction, and even curtailment of the use of credit by consumers, the cyclical effects of the interest rates have been such as to forestall any secular change in the measured saving rate. Only a return to high economic activity and selective, intentional discrimination in credit policy and tax policy toward investment is likely to move the relative percentages. It is much more likely that the general personal tax reductions of 1982 and 1983 will have been found to stimulate consumption rather than saving; indeed, virtually all forecasters contended that the consumption effects of the July 1982 tax reduction would mark the beginning of escape from recession. The tough, effective choices are for less dogmatic dependence on the aggregate supply of credit, moderate control of consumer credit extensions after recovery is well-footed, and a serious effort to redirect the personal tax system toward consumption rather than income.

Notes on an Industrial Policy

"Industrial policy" is a loose term; it means very different things in the hands of different writers and in different countries. I take it to mean governmental policies (a) that attempt to accelerate healthy adjustments in markets that would otherwise be achieved only over a painfully prolonged period; (b) that seek to achieve outcomes that markets cannot hope to achieve under existing laws (for example, the antitrust laws); (c) that underwrite, by guarantee or by actual carrying of the costs, outcomes that markets themselves will not produce under any circumstances; and (d) that seek to counteract the effects of industrial policies pursued by some of our trading partners, without resorting to overt protectionism. An effective "industrial policy" is activist; it calls for reviewing laws that stand in the way of industrial progress and for the actual provision of some capital, in one form or another, to accelerate industrial and technological development for domestic or international reasons.

The United States has virtually nothing in the way of a coherent industrial policy; unlike most of our international competitors, we tend to leave the market adjustment process alone, even if it is moving at a perilously slow rate and even if it exposes us to gross inefficiencies and painful unemployment.

Much of U.S. heavy industry—the steel industry can serve as a well-recognized illustration—is in deep trouble by its own ad-mission. Steel products are still produced by hundreds of com-panies, the vast majority of them below efficient size. Even the large companies are unable to justify the substantial investment required to elevate their efficiency; much of their own facilities are already fully written off, and the market is divided among too many participants (including Japanese and even European companies exporting into the U.S. market). Equilibrium eco-nomics says that all this will be taken care of in due course. The steel industry will shrink, and the least efficient will disappear; prices will then strengthen, and investment opportunities will arise. Some argue that even a high value-added, technological industry such as steel should be surrendered to import competition if it cannot or will not meet the competition (even if the competi-tion is subsidized by some other country's industrial policy).

But the adjustment process is agonizingly slow, and some of the necessary capital may be diverted through acquisition of com-panies in other industries. In the meantime, the United Kingdom, and all of Europe, and Japan have consolidated, integrated, and may soon be investing in modern facilities with the cooperative help of government capital (or quasi capital in the form of tax benefits).

In the oil industry, the market would doubtless, in the end, produce some alternative fuels for "energy independence," but the news on that front is not good, and for entirely expectable reasons; the risks are very large, and projections of the oil price, which enter into risk-reward calculations, are very uncertain. If there were to be an important national public purpose in the de-velopment of an alternative to conventional oil as an energy source, the market may not serve the purpose in time.

These simple illustrations could be multiplied in a number of basic American industries and even in some technologically ad-vanced industries. World-wide recession magnifies the threat; other countries are far more committed to the maintenance of employment than we are, and the resulting output affects our trade position in these and third markets.

This issue is not simply picking winners and losers for govern-ment assistance. An industrial policy should aim at the reinforce-ment of investment trends where there is a clear consensus of need; it should take an administrative form resistant to simple appeals for help from any one quarter. In some degree, it would displace the violent and often uneconomic competition among state and local governments to attract investment. It would represent, at best, a national effort to supplement market forces in stimulating and shaping the future capital stock.

An industrial policy runs the real risk of government mistakes in order to get the reward of fast adjustment and modernization. Its popularity world-wide reflects a growing awareness that in an increasingly competitive technological age time is short for some industries, and market processes too slow, too risk-laden, or too late in starting (or too assisted elsewhere) for private capital to succeed alone.

The issue of adopting an "industrial policy" is very large in the United States—bigger than elsewhere because the traditional posture of business and government toward each other has been negative for so long. On this issue, American pragmatism fails. Economists rest on the pure view that markets will do everything that should be done; if a market does not do it, it should not be done, by definition.

My own impression is that the risks are worth taking. Indeed, there are large risks in not supplementing markets—risks to the markets themselves. Almost uniformly among our principal trading competitors, the powers and resources of government are increasingly being used to foster growth and technological acceleration. There is a large risk in denying ourselves the power to accelerate industrial adjustment. The policy should deliberately minimize the displacement of competition as a controlling force over the capital stock. The subject of industrial policy offers the ultimate illustration of the conflict between timeless economic theory and exigent conditions—a conflict difficult for a society with powerful doctrinal positions on free enterprise and free markets. The 1980s will test our ability to leaven doctrine with pragmatism.

Human Resources for the 1980s

Almost no one would deny that the United States suffers from something that might be vaguely called a problem in human resources and that it better make some progress on the problem in the 1980s.

It is a many-sided problem incorporating the position of minorities in the system, the quality and effects of social programs that reduce the incentive to work, the educational system and the direction it should take for the 1980s, and the loud and clear call of the industrial system for a far higher level of technical training than we now achieve. Each of these subjects is a specialty in itself; each provides opportunity for a separate chapter. But it is fair to say that human resources will gradually come to dominate inputs into the economic system and that we have neither effective policy nor effective practice, nor even a reasoned objective, with respect to all of these issues. It need hardly be added that we are much more in need of such reasoned policies, by virtue of our ethnically pluralist work force, than the far more homogeneous nations with which we share the history of the mixed economy.

In general, in all of these areas except education, we have engaged in *postmarket* distributions, redistributing the income rewards of participating in the mainstream of U.S. economic activity. All of the welfare systems (including, in a special way, Social Security itself) rest largely on compassion, not economics. They represent the soft ethic of redistribution which we could afford when general living standards were rising rapidly in earlier postwar decades. Much of the redistribution system developed in the postwar years has been actually antieconomic, in the sense that it reduces incentives to work and even today penalizes the working poor.

What the human resources problem seems to call for is substantial *premarket* distribution—the redistribution of economic opportunity, not of economic results. Premarket distribution calls for a hard achievement ethic, not a soft distribution ethic, but it will require substantial and high-quality resources dedicated to formal and technical education and technical training. It will have to equip individuals psychologically, as well as in terms of job training, to earn their way in the work force and, by earning their way, to be in a position to forego the postmarket distribution. The very volume of postmarket redistribution in the United States is evidence of a failure to achieve a broader distribution of what is needed to achieve within the market. Given the present pace of technology, particularly information technology, the race is getting faster.

It is probable that a very heavy cost lies ahead in this area. The distribution of the problem is such that state and local efforts are unlikely to be suitable; it will take the cooperation of federal government and the private sector. In this area, the hard ethic of the 1980s will have to resist the pressures of the soft-ethic re-distribution philosophy; the objective is not just compassionate redistribution, but the preparation of the labor force to meet needs foreseeable five, ten, and twenty years out. The disciplining of soft-ethic distributive programs may well be warranted, but there will be plenty to do with whatever funds are saved. The abandonment of a federal education department seems not just unwarranted, but an abandonment of a crucial responsibility. Another ten years of the intensification of technology, together with a failure of American education and training to yield the educated workers technology will require, threatens to produce a growing under-class, endlessly in need of postmarket redistri-bution.

Starting from where we are, this may be the most impressive challenge of the 1980s. Investment in human resources is not even counted as investment in our conventional statistics. The challenge bears directly on President Reagan's uneasy question: why are there so many unemployed when the newspapers are full of want ads?

Concluding Comment

The subjects covered here, and the views taken, carry the suggestion that in the 1980s a federal government that in some respects is more activist, rather than less activist, will be required if U.S. economic performance is to improve at home and hold its own in international competition. It does *not* call for a larger government sector. But it does call for more rather than less government *power*—more selective monetary powers, less constric-tive fiscal principles, and some degree of involvement of govern-ment in the course of tangible and human investment. It calls for a reduction of the dogmatic isolation of government from the realities of the marketplace which has driven it inevitably into the role of a gigantic and growing transfer agent. It argues that the soft ethic of redistribution of income should be gradually displaced by a hard ethic that will provide new energy for private industry and a better educated and trained work force to fill the jobs. It calls for affirmative government, paying less attention to static economic principles and more attention to the human and industrial conditions that produce economic growth.

2

America in a Competitive Economic World

The immediate American problems are productivity growth and inflation, but they need to be seen in a broader context. For many years following World War II, the U.S. enjoyed "effortless superiority." We had a per capita gross national product (GNP) far above that of anyone else. Technologically, we had a huge lead in almost everything. As late as 1960 only 5 percent of the GNP was imported, and international trade could have been abolished without any major harm to the standard or style of life of the average American. America could afford activities and mistakes that no one else could afford.

The "effortless superiority" has disappeared. Economically and technologically, the U.S. is simply one among equals, and our rate of progress, productivity growth, is well below that of our major economic competitors. Imports have risen to 12 percent of the GNP, and the country is importing necessities such as oil.

While it is a shock to be simply one among equals, it is also

LESTER C. THUROW *is professor of economics and management at the Massachusetts Institute of Technology. He is a contributing editor at* Newsweek *and an economics columnist for several domestic and international publications. Mr. Thurow has been published in over thirty books and was the editor or author of eleven of them. His most recent effort is* Five Economic Challenges *(with Robert Heilbroner).*

more pleasant to live in a neighborhood with other wealthy countries. To catch up, other countries obviously had to have an extended period of time when they grew faster than the United States. But there inevitably comes a time, and it is now, when the U.S. has to accelerate its economic performance to keep up with the rest of the industrial world.

In the abstract, everyone sings the praises of competition and being in a competitive market. For the first time in a long time the U.S. is now in a competitive world, and most Americans are not going to like it since the competition will require some fundamental changes in hallowed American practices and traditions. In a competitive environment, one can be beaten.

There is no turning back to the "good old days." Before or after the New Deal, the U.S. has never had the sustained productivity gains now being achieved by Japan, France, or Germany. To keep up in the future, the United States is going to have to develop new institutions and new ways of accelerating economic growth. Things that "can't" be done will have to be done if we are not to decline relative to the rest of the world.

The Competition

Basically America has not been in a competitive world since we surpassed Great Britain in per capita GNP at the turn of the century. But after World War II the U.S. had a huge economic and technological lead on everyone in almost everything. This lead has now evaporated, and the U.S. is essentially where Great Britain was at the turn of the century. Other countries have caught up, and their current rate of productivity growth is higher than ours. If the trends continue, the U.S. standard of living will fall below that of the most advanced industrial countries. Our problem is not to regain the old lead—that is probably both impossible and undesirable—but to attain a rate of growth of productivity that allows us to run even with the leaders of the industrial pack. If we do not, our economy will follow the trail blazed by the British whose average standard of living is now approximately half that of the industrial leaders.

If the current trend is allowed to continue, the consequences are severe. U.S. citizens experience a falling relative (and perhaps absolute) standard of living. America gradually becomes incapable of bearing the military burden implicit in leading the democratic industrial countries. Alliances will be rearranged and someone else will take over our role, but the changeover is apt to be disruptive. There certainly is not a natural successor the way there was when the U.S. replaced Great Britain as the leading democratic power. Japan and Germany may have leading economies, but their history makes it difficult for them to take political, diplomatic, and military leadership.

In regaining our industrial dynamism we have one advantage and one disadvantage. Our advantage is that we have not yet been clearly surpassed. We do not have a lot of catching up to do. Depending upon exactly how it is measured, average U.S. productivity is either slightly above or slightly below that of the leading countries in Europe. No one finds a significant gap either way. Relative to the average level of productivity in Japan, the U.S. still has a substantial lead, but this is misleading since the Japanese average basically covers two economies—a highly inefficient domestic service and farming economy and a highly efficient export-oriented manufacturing economy. Many of the export-oriented Japanese industries have productivity better than that of their American counterparts.

While it is true that with flexible exchange rates a less efficient economy can be competitive and have a comparative advantage in the sense that it can export to a more efficient economy, absolute efficiency is still important. If we systematically fall behind in absolute efficiency and no longer are the world leader in technology, then our economy is forced to shift away from what should be high-income opportunities to concentrate on low-income areas of the economy where we do have a comparative advantage. This leads to falling income or a slower rate of growth of income than in the leading countries and probably has severe social consequences if you are used to being a leading industrial country. Self-confidence and the willingness to compete disappear when a country cannot be competitive in new economic activities. Economically, a country becomes a less interesting country. Think of the brain drain that has occurred from Great Britain because the best scientists and engineers see that their ideas can best be used elsewhere and that their individual opportunities are better elsewhere.

Our disadvantage is that the U.S. rate of growth of productivity is now far below that of our competitors, has been falling since 1965, and in absolute terms is now lower than it was four years ago. If the decline in productivity is examined on an industry by industry basis, there are a number of industries where a slowdown in productivity growth is permanent. This means that to return to our old rate of growth of productivity some *new* sources of productivity growth are going to have to be found. The U.S. cannot go back to the "good old days" because the "good old days" are permanently gone.

THE DECLINE IN PRODUCTIVITY

Productivity growth is like a gold mine. Some smart or lucky prospector finds a vein of high-grade ore that is then followed down into the bowels of the earth. But eventually every vein of ore peters out. To keep the same or an increasing volume of gold coming out of the mine, new veins of ore must continually be found. Similarly the cessation of American productivity growth cannot be traced to stupid or lazy miners. Old low-grade veins of productivity ore simply have not been replaced with new high-grade finds.

For example, when American productivity was growing at 3 percent per year, the productivity of electrical and gas utilities was growing at more than 6 percent per year. Utility productivity is now falling at the rate of 1 percent per year. This change alone explains 10 percent of the slowdown in American productivity. What happened?

The answer is simple. In utilities, most of the hours of work are involved in maintaining the distribution network. As long as every home and factory is demanding more energy, productivity rises rapidly. More kilowatts are being delivered, but the same number of hours are needed to maintain the distribution network. But, conversely, when the demand for energy goes down because energy prices are up, the same number of hours are needed to maintain the lines, and productivity falls.

The utility productivity problem is not curable. Some other new source of productivity growth must be found to offset the declining productivity in utilities. Other sources of the decline, such as the decline in mining productivity, the end of the shift out of agriculture, and the rapid growth of services are of a similar character. They cannot be cured. New sources of productivity growth must be found. *In toto,* 30 to 40 percent of the decline in U.S. productivity can be traced to such permanent factors.

The Reagan administration has focused on inadequate investment as the sole cause of the productivity problem. Most studies only trace 20 to 25 percent of the productivity slowdown to inadequate investment, but the problem is not that the Americans are investing less. While productivity was growing at more than 3 percent per year from 1948 to 1965, Americans were investing 9.5 percent of the GNP in private plant and equipment. While productivity was falling at the rate of 0.3 percent per year from 1977 to 1981, Americans invested 11.3 percent of the GNP in private plant and equipment. Investment went up 20 percent while productivity died. Why?

The solution to the puzzle is simple. Because of the baby boom twenty years ago, the labor force is growing very rapidly. Plant and equipment per worker is falling even though the capital stock is growing faster. With a falling capital to labor ratio, falling productivity is no great surprise. But the solution is not to return to some virtuous past when Americans invested more (there never was such a past) but to raise American investment to levels that it has never achieved.

Thus the U.S. is going to require very large new sources of productivity growth to get back to our historic 3 percent rate of growth of productivity and even larger new sources to obtain the levels of productivity growth enjoyed by major competitors.

The Need to Compete

At the same time as the world is becoming competitive, the U.S. is entering an era where it is more important for us to be able to compete. In 1960, the U.S. imported 5 percent of the GNP. In 1981, we imported 12 percent of the GNP—not far below the Japanese percentage. Whereas we imported few necessities in

1960, today we import many necessities. As a result, the U.S. has to learn to be export-oriented in a way that it has never been export-oriented.

Here again with flexible exchange rates we can always compete with a comparative advantage in farm products, raw materials, or on the basis of lower wages than that of our major competitors, but I do not think that the U.S. wants to compete on the basis of relatively low wages. If we are to have a standard of living equal to that of the world's leaders, we have to be able to compete not only in the leading edge of industrial products, but we also have to be just as good at selling to the rest of the world as the Japanese are today.

This means being willing to design products for non-American customers, being willing to make major investments to penetrate foreign markets, and being willing to learn foreign languages and customs. American firms cannot expect to compete under American rules in foreign markets. They will have to be willing to compete under the local rules and customs.

While the U.S. will not generate a high standard of living depending upon farm exports alone, the competitive nature of the current world economy and America's need to compete means that we can no longer tolerate the agricultural protection that Japan and the Common Market give their farmers. If they will not open their agricultural markets (one of our major comparative advantages), then we should close them off from some of their major comparative advantages in our markets. We simply cannot afford to continue our current generosity in agricultural trade.

The Inflation Problem

Before dealing with the structural factors necessary to restart healthy economic growth, it is necessary to find a cure for the inflation problem. The current policy of stopping economic growth to force inflation out of the economy simply is not viable in the long run. As long as such policies are in place it is simply impossible to do the restructuring necessary to solve our long-run competitive problem.

In the 1970s all of the industrial countries (some consistently, some fitfully) brought economic growth to a halt with tight monetary policies designed to stop inflation. With Japan slipping into negative economic growth in the fourth quarter of 1981, the industrial world managed to stop economic growth everywhere. This has created an economic crisis, but a crisis that is self-imposed. Our problems are not due to sun spots or oil shocks, but due to the fact that everyone has attempted to stop inflation with no growth.

Whatever your beliefs about the validity of this effort, it is clear that its viability has come to an end. The 1980s will have to be a decade of restarting economic growth. If inflation is to be fought, some other technique will have to be found. The current economic and political system simply cannot stand another decade of the present economic policies.

Mixed economies do not work very well without growth. In the last decade unemployment has risen toward 10 percent in both the United States and the Common Market. Can anyone really imagine it rising toward 20 percent in the next decade? Youth unemployment is enormous everywhere, but it rises toward 50 percent among American black teenagers—up to 90 percent in our central city ghettos. How are we going to economically absorb our children if present policies continue?

With stagnation, protection is breaking out everywhere. It is clear that continuing on the current course is going to lead to a world broken into trading blocks just as it was in the 1930s. With protection, Third World countries are not going to break into development. If you look at the countries that have become developed countries—starting with Europe after World War II and continuing with Hong Kong, Singapore, South Korea, and Taiwan —all developing countries need to go through a period where their exports rise very rapidly. But with protection and no growth in the developed countries, that is impossible. As a result we are not going to have the Third World success stories in the 1980s that we had in the 1970s.

Consider our industrial structure. In the first quarter of 1982, the real American GNP was at the same level as three years earlier in the first quarter of 1979. Where has that left us? Think of the firms that are essentially bankrupt—International Harvester; Pan American, Braniff, and Continental Airlines; Chrysler. Optimists see 500 savings and loan banks going broke in the next year; pessimists see 1,000. Net farm income is down more than 50 percent with widespread bankruptcies. Corporate profits look good in America, but only because of the oil companies who are capturing all of the profits. Eight of the largest ten firms in America are now oil companies. As the process of no growth continues, our industrial structures get weaker and weaker and weaker. At some point the structure is going to collapse.

Simple money supply monetarism is a triumph of faith over evidence. The faith holds that tight money will stop inflation without stopping the economy. The evidence indicates otherwise. In the Great Depression unemployment rose to 25 percent in the United States—yet real wages continued to rise throughout the period. Prices fell 25 percent, but only from 1929 to 1933. After that the economic collapse even ceased reducing prices. American unemployment is now rising toward 10 percent. What evidence do we have that tight money will stop inflation without wrecking our economies?

Think of an analogy. Suppose I were to drop a feather from the highest building in Boston. What do I know because of the law of gravity? The feather will eventually hit the ground. But there is another story to tell about the feather. If the wind is blowing, the feather may go up—not down. It may stay up for a very long time and when it lands be far from the bottom of the building. None of this repeals the law of gravity, but it does say that there is another story to be told.

Monetarism is like the law of gravity. If monetary growth is stopped long enough and hard enough, inflation will stop. At some point all economic activity, including inflation, stops. But it takes a very long time with an enormous price. A price so large that it is not obvious that our social and industrial structures could, would, or should pay it.

We have to rebuild our economies so that they can withstand another oil shock without having to stop economic growth for a half decade after each shock. Such a shock may not occur in the future, but no one should plan on it. Plans have to be based on the likelihood of other inflationary shocks—if not from oil, then from something else.

We all know what must be done. Consider the simple arithmetic of oil shocks in the United States. Because of OPEC oil shock I and II, the percentage of the American GNP that went to imported oil rose from 1 percent in 1972 to 5 percent in 1980. This means that wages and all other forms of income must go down 4 percent if inflation is to be avoided. In the United States ten cents out of every consumption dollar goes directly or indirectly to purchase energy. This means that if energy prices rise 100 percent, then all other prices must fall 11 percent to preserve a noninflationary environment. But if prices are to fall 11 percent outside of the energy areas, all wages and incomes generated outside of the energy area must also fall 11 percent.

There is a simple problem. How is the message to be delivered? Prices can go up faster than wages, and other incomes, or government can stop the economy, raise unemployment, and attempt to force incomes down. But when the message is delivered with no growth and high unemployment, it seems to take a very long time to be heard—so long, that the message is more economically painful than the inflationary disease it is trying to cure.

In the 1980s vigorous economic growth must be restarted. We know how to do that—Lord Keynes taught us. If we are to fight inflation at the same time, however, we must design a strategy for doing so that does not shut down our economies at the same time.

Here we know what must be done, but not how to do it. Wage and price flexibility must be built into the economy to cope with supply-side shocks. The key words are "income policies," "social contracts," "wage flexibility." The preferred option is to create more wage flexibility rather than to attempt to stop inflation with systems of rules and regulations or consensus (something that is virtually impossible in an economy as large as that of the U.S.).

Elsewhere I have suggested that some fraction of wages—maybe 33 percent—should be tied to some measure of firm or plant productivity. Value added is, I think, the right measure, but the problem at this point is not to work out the technical details but to begin at least an intellectual movement to legitimize the idea that wages (and other incomes) can be flexible. Such a system would help us cope with inflation and might also help motivate American workers to take a greater interest in productivity.

Politically you might tell me that it cannot be done and therefore working out the technical problems is a waste of time. I agree.

It cannot now be done. But it must be done. We have to make it politically possible or we will not have a viable economy.

"Destroying the village to save the village" is not a good military, political, or economic strategy. Yet that is precisely the strategy upon which we have embarked for the past decade. It is ultimately a losing strategy, and we are losing.

Building a Structure Capable of Competing

No one can build a high-quality economy out of low-quality components. But this dictum applies just as much to the human component going into the economy as it does the investment component.

Six out of every ten people who take the New York Telephone Company's competency test flunk it. Until 1981 the average test score on the Scholastic Aptitude Test—the test given to college bound seniors—had fallen for eighteen consecutive years. The test score in 1981 did not go up, but at least it did not go down. No one knows whether this is the bottom or a temporary pause in the route to illiteracy. The economy is perpetually short of skilled blue-collar workers such as machinists or tool and die makers. With major military build-up underway, the shortages will increase from being acute to being critical. On a per capita basis we produce half as many engineers as Japan. Science education is collapsing in our schools as science and math teachers leave for better job opportunities in industry.

With a low-quality, untrained labor force, how is America to compete in a scientific world filled with economic competitors who are our equals financially and technologically? To do nothing is to commit national economic suicide.

Yet the Reagan administration is dismantling the education and training programs of the federal government. Many of them were severely slashed in 1981 and 1982. All of the physical investment in the world will not help the American economy unless we have a labor force well-educated enough to use the sophisticated tools of tomorrow.

Any particular manpower program can be labeled a failure and abandoned, but manpower programs in general cannot be abandoned. The economy needs the skills that are not being produced. The individuals who are not being trained remain part of society. In the era of robots, what is to become of a functionally illiterate, unskilled, high school dropout? One can be hard-nosed about poverty and illiteracy, but the hard-nosed fact is that these unskilled people are going to be part of our society for the rest of their lives. And their children may carry on where they left off. In the education and training area, every failure simply has to be replaced with another attempt until a successful approach is found.

Government responsibility for education and training was established more than a hundred years before the New Deal. Social welfare programs may be a matter of ethics and generosity, but education and training are not. I pay taxes to help educate my neighbor's children not because I am generous, but because I cannot afford to live with them uneducated. And since people can vote with their feet, as the President recently suggested they do, the federal government cannot afford to leave education and training to either private individuals or state and local governments.

It is strange that an administration pledged to supply-side economics designed to speed up economics and praising the virtues of individualism seems to think that the human component is unimportant when it comes to success. But whatever the cause of this psychological quirk, it is not a quirk with which the country can afford to live.

The same problem is now visible in our civilian research and development spending. As a percent of GNP we are now spending less than our competitors. In the past we spent a higher fraction of the GNP and were multiplying that fraction by a much larger per capita GNP. How is a cutback to strengthen American efforts?

There is also a major weakness in the allocation of effort. Most money and talent goes into developing new products rather than into process research and development. Yet process research and development are precisely where the greatest payoffs are to be found, since it takes a long time for a new product to have a major impact on an economy as large as that of the U.S. This bias partly comes about because of the ways in which we allocate scientific prestige and what has paid off in the past when we did not have competitors who could make our products 15 percent cheaper, but it has also come about because of the adversarial relationship between government and industry. Almost by definition, process research and development have to be done in industry. But this means that federally funded process research and development funds look like direct subsidies to particular industries or firms. Yet firms will not undertake the efforts alone, because they cannot capture all of the benefits. Perhaps the answer is to be found in partially federally funded cooperative research and development projects where everyone can participate if they are willing to pay some of the cost. Changes in the antitrust laws clearly to permit cooperative research and development would also help. But whatever the answer, an answer must be found.

INSTITUTIONAL CHANGES

There are going to have to be institutional changes as well as efforts to increase the quantity of physical capital and the quality of human capital. Other successful economies are marked by aggressive investment banking—usually government backed. For all practical purposes the U.S. does not have investment banks. There are institutions, such as Morgan Stanley, bearing the name, but none of them has major amounts of money that can be committed to long-run investments. They are instead middlemen between potential industrialists and investors.

The problem is now visible in the auto industry. Because of Japanese competition, auto producers cannot raise prices to finance needed investment. But without the new investment they will not be able to build a competitive car to fend off the Japanese. Unless some new technique can be found for infusing the industry with capital, it will simply go out of business. But autos are not a sunset industry that America can afford to discard.

Compare what is going on in the auto industry with what did go on at Mazda after the 1973–1974 oil shock. Mazda had been gearing up to conquer the auto world with the rotary engine car. It might have succeeded, but the price of gasoline went up, and the one weakness of the rotary engine car was its bad fuel mileage. Suddenly, the company's sales plunged, and it was for all intents and purposes broke. What happened? The banking system (government) absorbed much of the losses on the economically obsolete rotary engine plants, and the firm was lent billions of dollars to redesign and retool for a conventional piston engine car. After a number of years the company was able to turn the situation around and once again became a powerful competitor in the auto business. But during the interim period, the company was carried by the banking system. What would have happened to Mazda in the U.S.?

A similar problem is visible in steel. The steel industry probably should go out of business as a producer of hundreds of millions of tons of raw pig iron, but it ought to be rejuvenated as a high technology steel industry. The industry might be much smaller, but it would still play an important role in the U.S. industrial life. How is this to come about in the context of foreign competition and a "big" steel industry that is clearly interested in getting out of steel. "Mini" steel mills will play an important role, but there is also probably room for a new integrated "big" steel mill to produce the products that cannot be produced in "mini" steel mills. If such a mill cost $3.5 billion, how is it to be financed? U.S. Steel put the money that it had set aside for a new steel mill into Marathon Oil.

The semiconductor industry is on the edge of the same problem. The industry is shifting from low capital-intensive technologies to much higher levels of capital intensity. At the same time it is in competition with Japanese firms. The normal American way to finance the necessary shifts in technology would be to accumulate internal savings from current profits to finance the plants necessary to produce the products of the future. But with competition that holds prices down and does not need current savings to finance plants for future expansion, there is no way that the traditional American pattern can work. To rely on it is simply to give up the semiconductor industry to the Japanese.

Consider robots. Why do the Japanese have 66 percent of all of the robots in the world? The answer is clear. One, they save enough to afford them, but, two, the government has played an active role in promoting the use of robots. What problem do you have if you are a producer of robots? It is difficult to sell enough robots initially to get the overhead economies that permit low per unit cost. What problems do you have if you are a potential buyer of robots? You are not sure how productive they will be and if you can repair them. You want to buy one or two to experiment, but not very many. MITI and the Japanese banking system stepped into this situation to organize a government-backed leasing company. The company guaranteed the producers sales of a certain level and leased the robots on a short-run basis to industry. No overt cost subsidies were given, but the leasing company took much of the risk. If robots had not worked, it would have been left with millions of dollars in unusable robots. Social actions were taken to reduce private risk. This is essentially the role that industrial policy should take.

Society should not subsidize the private sector, but it should take actions to lower private risks.

But the real case for private and public investment banks is not even that we need them, but that we are gradually creating an inefficient system of congressional investment banking. It should be replaced with a more efficient and overt system of investment banking that organizes a sharing of the risks without the political pressures of congressional special-interest groups.

Think of recent congressional investment banking actions. Lockheed and Chrysler are two examples of congressional investment banking designed to bail out failing companies. The Alaskan natural gas pipeline act was an example of congressional investment banking designed to get a large project underway. The hundreds of bills of off-budget government loan guarantees are essentially congressional investment banking. Whatever you think about the rights and wrongs of these actions, it is clear that we need a different mechanism for dealing with the demands that lead to those congressional actions.

To be against private and public investment banking is simply to be in favor of a highly politicized and inefficient congressional investment banking system.

The solutions are as clear as they are difficult to implement. Liberals cringe at the thought of consumption taxes and a nationwide banking system where the small town bank is a thing of the past. Conservatives do not like the idea of the government as one of the country's major savers or that government-backed investment banks will probably be necessary to compete with the government-backed investment banks that are aggressively pushing industrial development abroad. But both sides are going to have to do things they do not like, not because they want to, but because the foreign competition demands it.

The starting point is to alter banking and antitrust regulations to allow the formation of real private investment banks who have major amounts of their own resources that they can devote to industrial investments. The current financial mergers are headed in this direction anyway, but they need to be directed with changes in rules and regulations toward investment banking rather than more elaborate systems of consumer finance. The U.S. does not need a better banking system for servicing the consumer. In some sense—low savings rates and high usage of consumer credit—we have a banking system that is too good when it comes to servicing the consumer. The U.S. needs patient long-run investment funds.

In addition to making the necessary changes to allow real investment banks to be formed, it will be necessary to make a couple of other changes if the system is to work to promote new industries. First, when it comes to representation on boards of directors, we need to collapse the distinction between debt and equity as the Germans have done. If an investment bank makes major long-run loans to an industrial firm, it deserves representation on its board of directors just as if it had made an equity investment. No investment bank is going to make major commitments unless it gets some "hands-on" management and information. Investment banks should be allowed to take a more active role in industrial management.

Second, there has to be an easy mechanism, as there is in Japan, for converting loans into equity. The combination of these two items would essentially prevent hostile takeover bids and stop management from having to manipulate quarterly profits to keep their stock market price-earnings multiples up and the chances of a hostile takeover down.

With the formation of real private investment banks, it would then be possible to see where the system of financing industry still remains weak. Those weaknesses will lead us into the appropriate role for public investment banking.

The U.S. now lives in a competitive economic world. Others are our equals financially and technologically. This means that the traditional method of financing industrial investment—internal savings generated out of current profits and depreciation allowances —is simply dead. The foreign competition does not finance their future investments in that pattern, and their pricing actions will stop us from financing our future investments with that pattern no matter how much we would like to continue using the "old ways." The challenge is to find new ways to finance the investments of the future.

Conclusion

President Carter was fond of referring to the energy problem as the moral equivalent of war. He was wrong. America's economic problems are not the moral equivalent of war; they are the moral equivalent of defeat. A defeat teaches everyone that the old ways do not work—they have just been defeated. New ways have to be tried. In some sense the U.S. has suffered an economic defeat and must respond with new ideas, institutions, and ways of operating.

What we need is similar to the American response to the Soviet sputnik. A relatively minor scientific defeat leads to a major effort to upgrade and improve U.S. scientific capabilities. The programs worked. Americans were the first to land on the moon. The question is whether we will respond to the current general economic problems in a positive way or let them slide by us as Great Britain has let its economic eclipse slide by it.

Rudolph G. Penner

3

Fiscal Management

Introduction

This chapter is primarily about creating and managing information flows. It is assumed that if better information is provided to policy makers and ultimately to the voter, fiscal management will be improved. The reader will probably quickly recognize the author's prejudice that imperfect information flows lead to an upward bias in spending. However, I doubt that a different prejudice would greatly affect the structure of the analysis. Better fiscal management can mean either wiser budget expansions or wiser budget cuts. It is only with better information that we can decide which should predominate.

RUDOLPH G. PENNER *is director of fiscal policy studies and a resident scholar at the American Enterprise Institute. Formerly assistant director for economic policy at the Office of Management and Budget, he has also served as deputy assistant secretary for economic affairs at the Department of Housing and Urban Development and as senior staff economist at the Council of Economic Advisers. Prior to 1975, Mr. Penner was a professor of economics at the University of Rochester. He has written a number of books and articles on tax and spending issues and contributes a monthly column to* The New York Times. *This chapter expands upon a lecture given by the author at the University of Kiel in West Germany. That lecture was titled "How to Reduce Government Growth: An American View" and will be published in* Reassessing the Role of Government in the Mixed Economy, *a conference volume edited by Herbert Giersch.*

It is not only necessary to create better information. That information has to be delivered to policy makers and voters in a relatively painless fashion. Policy makers are very busy people. They cannot be expected to wade through mountains of material.

The voters present a more difficult problem. Unless they are wise in their selection of candidates, their collective policy wishes are unlikely to be satisfied. But it is not in the voters' self-interests to spend much time studying complex public issues. In the jargon of public choice theory, it is quite reasonable for the voter to remain "rationally ignorant" about budget policy. The voters have no direct influence over that policy and are kept busy enough gathering the information necessary to make efficient private decisions. Consequently, their attitudes toward government are not well-defined and, as revealed in public opinion polls, often seem downright irrational. Poll after poll suggest that voters would like to see total spending and tax burdens reduced, and yet the same polls show a great reluctance to cut spending on specific federal programs such as defense, Social Security, education, etc. There is, of course, a desire to cut waste and fraud but, apparently, little understanding that some waste and fraud is optimum, since it often costs much more than a dollar's worth of management resources to reduce waste and fraud by a dollar.

Some polls show hostility to specific program areas such as foreign aid and agriculture, but these two items typically constitute less than 3 percent of total outlays. More recently, there has been considerable hostility toward "welfare." Again, few seem to recognize that, at the federal level, welfare is relatively unimportant. Outlays providing health, housing, nutrition, and cash assistance to the poor constitute less than 10 percent of total outlays, and, while there is some desire to cut these programs a bit, there is little support for altering them radically. Income-conditioned transfer payments are dwarfed by the cost of transfers and health services that are provided to rich and poor alike. Such assistance constitutes about 30 percent of the total federal budget, and its share is growing rapidly. The bulk of such assistance goes to the nonpoor elderly, and programs for the elderly are highly popular. Defense spending constitutes about 25 percent of outlays; with the disappearance of the hostility toward the military that was engendered by the Vietnam War and with the growing perception of the threat posed by the Soviets, increased defense spending has also gained strong public support.

In summary, attitudes toward total spending seem at best ambivalent and at worst confused. The generalized hostility toward government that aided the election of President Reagan may have its roots, as much or more, in the regulation and the policies of the government than in its spending policies. Since the early 1970s there has been an explosion of regulatory activity. Well-intentioned efforts to use regulation to improve the environment, to provide equal opportunity to minorities, and to insure worker health and safety have made government all intrusive and have imposed enormous costs on the private sector. At the same time a combination of tax bracket creep and legislative action raised marginal tax rates on the middle and upper-middle classes during the 1970s without significantly raising the revenue yield of the tax system. There was a growing perception that the income tax system was "unfair," and it made President Reagan's 1980 campaign promise to cut marginal tax rates highly popular. Unfortunately, public hostility toward taxes, combined with public ambivalence toward spending, led American politicians to cut taxes vigorously in the summer of 1981 while making only minor changes in spending programs.

This chapter will focus mainly on the problem of controlling spending growth at the federal level in the face of public ambivalence on the issue. While the voters often give contradicting signals to politicians on spending issues, there are other related difficulties with the way that democratic governments make spending decisions, and I believe that the result is very probably upwardly biased spending in the sense that the final outcome involves more spending than would be desired by the median voter. It is, in fact, the rational ignorance of the typical voter that opens the door to narrow special-interest groups who lobby for spending on their own favorite programs even though those programs have low benefit to cost ratios judged from the interest of society as a whole. This is a common theme of the public choice literature, and I have little doubt regarding its validity.

However, its implications may often be exaggerated. Wasteful programs, specifically designed for narrow special interests, cannot become too visible or else they will provoke a reaction from the general taxpayer. This very fact restrains their growth. While the U.S. budget contains many such programs for farmers, home builders, the merchant marine, energy producers, etc., they have not been responsible for much of the growth of the federal government relative to the gross national product (GNP). This does not mean that they do not present problems for they do involve much waste.

But the real problem involves not *narrow* special interests but *broad* special interests, and, as already suggested, the most difficult budget control issue in the United States involves dealing with the growing elderly population. The American Social Security System has 36 million recipients. Millions of others, who are related to the recipients, also have a direct interest in the system in that if benefits are reduced, they may have to bear greater financial responsibility for their elderly and disabled relatives. It is quite possible, and in fact probable, that those with a direct interest in the system constitute a majority of the voting population. How, in a democracy, can this majority be prevented from exploiting the minority? I do not have a satisfactory answer, but the issue will be explored in the last section of this chapter.

Dealing with defense spending is equally perplexing. There is majority voter support for a strong defense, but how is that to be achieved? The voter cannot possibly keep well-informed on complex defense issues. Again voter ignorance opens the door to narrow special interests who would like to sell whatever weapons systems they happen to produce. This difficult problem will be considered in the last section along with programs for the elderly. Since defense and elderly programs will constitute about 60 percent of the budget in the next few years, it is hard to imagine overall federal budget control in the U.S. without contending with these two issues.

Before dealing with these two difficult areas in detail, more generalized budget control techniques will be examined. But prior to that, it is useful to examine recent trends in spending levels at all levels of government in the United States.

Table 1 illustrates the experience of the last twenty-six years. There is a strong upward trend in total government outlays between 1955 and 1975 with some flattening since that time. That flattening is, in part, due to the effects of the business cycle, but

TABLE 1. GOVERNMENT EXPENDITURES COMPARED TO THE GROSS NATIONAL
PRODUCT

| | | *(Billions of Dollars)* | | | | | |
| | | Total Government | | Federal | | State & Local | |
Year	GNP	Amount	% of GNP	Amount	% of GNP	Amount	% of GNP
1955	$ 400.0	$ 98.0	24.5	$ 68.1	17.0	$ 32.9	8.2
1960	506.5	136.4	26.9	93.1	18.4	49.8	9.8
1965	691.1	187.8	27.2	123.8	17.9	75.1	10.9
1970	992.7	313.4	31.6	204.3	20.6	133.5	13.5
1975	1,549.2	534.3	34.5	356.6	23.0	232.2	15.0
1976	1,718.0	574.9	33.5	384.8	22.4	251.2	14.6
1977	1,918.0	624.0	32.5	421.5	22.0	270.0	14.1
1978	2,156.1	681.9	31.6	460.7	21.4	298.4	13.8
1979	2,413.9	753.2	31.2	509.2	21.1	324.4	13.4
1980	2,626.1	869.0	33.1	602.0	22.9	355.0	13.5
1981	2,925.5	979.7	33.5	688.4	23.5	380.5	13.0

the most dramatic development shown by the table involves state and local spending. In relative terms, state and local budgets grew much more rapidly than the federal budget over the same period. That relative growth came to a screeching halt in the middle 1970s. Between 1975 and 1981 state and local spending grew only 1 percent per year in excess of the GNP deflator.

One can only speculate on the causes of this drastic change. Demography probably explains a large part of the phenomenon. Between 35 and 40 percent of total state and local expenditures are related to education. The significant fall in birth rates during the 1960s reduced this burden.

However, other factors also played a role. The tax revolt hit state and local governments before it affected the federal government. It was manifested in the electorate passing constitutional limits on tax burdens in many states, but this was just a symptom of a more widespread movement which led politicians to restrain spending and tax burdens even in states in which no new constitutional limits were passed.

Control over grants-in-aid from the federal to state and local government also played a role in curbing state and local spending. After growing from 0.7 percent of the GNP in 1955 to 3.5 percent in 1975, they leveled off, and many of the Carter administration's budget-cutting efforts were concentrated in this area. By 1981, grants had fallen relatively to 3 percent of the GNP and can be expected to fall further in the Reagan administration.

Institutional Responses to the Budget Problem

THE OFFICE OF MANAGEMENT AND BUDGET (OMB)

Since the 1920s the formidable task of putting together the President's budget has fallen to the Office of Management and Budget (known as the Bureau of the Budget prior to the Nixon administration). Prior to the 1920s each department submitted budget requests to Congress separately. There are well over a thousand defense, international, and domestic programs that should be considered, and, in the perfect world of the economist, spending increases or decreases in each program would be traded off against increases or decreases in all of the others. But that would imply the analysis of well over a million trade-offs, and there is no humanly possible way of accomplishing that much work every year or every decade for that matter.

Only a tiny portion of the entire universe of issues can be considered in detail every year, and the procedures of OMB must be designed, first, to identify the issues which should be raised, and, second, to bring to bear all of the available information relevant to the resolution of the issues. Since only a small portion of the whole can be considered carefully every year, it is extremely difficult to make significant changes in either the composition or the overall trend of spending in a short period of time. One of the most radical shifts in national priorities occurred with the election of President Reagan in 1980, and an unusually large number of program changes occurred in the summer of 1981. However, some future historian armed only with budget data and no other information might have trouble deciding whether anything special happened in 1981. The share of the federal government in GNP will remain about the same over the next few years. The composition of spending will shift somewhat toward defense, but if our mythical historian did some more digging, he or she would find that this change occurred in the early 1980s mainly because of decisions taken in the Carter administration. It will take until the middle 1980s for the Reagan priorities to have a substantial impact on the budget.

In order to begin implementing a President's priorities as soon as possible within these stringent constraints, OMB has evolved an elaborate set of procedures which has served them well over the years. The process begins in the spring for the budget which will be submitted the following January, which in turn develops presidential recommendations for the fiscal year beginning October 1. In the so-called spring review, the director of OMB seeks to identify the major issues which must be considered through the rest of the year. On the basis of this review the director advises the President on the overall budget strategy, and the President decides on a total spending target and allocates that sum among the departments. This is typically done by early summer.

The departments respond by submitting their own budget requests. Needless to say, a large portion of the departments' requests is devoted to explaining why they cannot live within the targets formulated by the President. In early fall, the departments defend their requests in hearings organized by OMB staff. The hearings are adversarial with OMB attempting to find weaknesses in the pro-spending arguments of the departments.

The department budget requests and the results of these hearings are reviewed by the OMB director and staff in the fall, and at that time the director decides on the detailed recommendations he will give to the President. During the hearings and director's review, OMB would like to have available objective program evaluations which would help to identify particularly inefficient programs. A subsequent section of this chapter identifies various attempts to force the bureaucracy into making such evaluations, but, as will be noted there, the attempts have not been very effective.

Note that the OMB director comes to the President with his recommendations first; this gives him great power. Cabinet members can appeal the President's decisions, but appeals take time, and time is a scarce commodity for any President. A cabinet member who wastes the President's time on secondary issues will not be very popular. Therefore, a wise cabinet member will restrict appeals to a very few high priority issues, leaving much of the rest of the field to the OMB director.

The President is forced to rely heavily on OMB, because it is one of the few places in government which provides arguments for not spending money. A President, regardless of his ideology, desperately needs such arguments since there is no way that all of the demands of the departments can be satisfied. It is sometimes said that a President relies on OMB for "neutral competence." I think that this is misleading. The OMB director and staff are not neutral. They are strong advocates. They almost always argue for less spending on everything. But they are competent. Over its history OMB has managed to attract the elite of the civil service.

THE CONGRESSIONAL BUDGET PROCESS

In the early 1970s, President Nixon became frustrated by his inability to control spending through Congress. To bring the matter to a head, he began to refuse to spend appropriated money on social programs. Such presidential impoundments had a long history even though it had never been clearly determined whether or not they were constitutional. However, President Nixon used this power more vigorously than previous Presidents.

The impoundments were challenged in the courts, but before the issue could be settled, Congress began to legislate restrictions on the President's power. Nixon effectively responded that Congress had no mechanism for controlling spending itself and it was inappropriate for Congress to restrict presidential power.

Since the late nineteenth century, Congress had been making tax and spending decisions quite separately, and spending was determined by a number of different committees without any vote ever taken on total spending, total receipts, or the implied deficit. Congress knew that Nixon had the better side of the argument, and they reacted by creating a new congressional budget process in 1974 while, at the same time, creating explicit procedures through which a President could impound funds.

I shall not describe the complex details of these procedures since such descriptions are readily available elsewhere. The important point is that Congress had to vote on spending, tax, and deficit totals explicitly. It was hoped that legislators would no longer be able to vote for expanding particular programs while continuing to preach in favor of lower taxes and deficits.

It is not easy to assess the degree of success of the new process. Needless to say, the procedure has not solved all of the budget problems, and it has, in fact, exhibited a number of weaknesses. For example, it greatly reduced the number of inconsistent votes by legislators. Their targets for total outlays and deficits have often been violated, and, more and more frequently, Congress has failed even to abide by the schedule for passing congressional budgets.

Yet, I believe that the procedure has been and will continue to be of considerable value. Inconsistent votes become very apparent and can, in theory, be used as evidence by opponents of incumbents. Because the process requires a five-year budget projection, the long-run implications of decisions are being made more explicit, and Congress has definitely lengthened its time horizon for making decisions. This has made the legislators more sensitive to the role of economic assumptions in determining future budget totals. While this initially resulted in the adoption of overly optimistic economic forecasts, those forecasts became somewhat more realistic in 1982.

In addition, the Congressional Budget Office, created to provide technical information for the implementation of the process, has over the years greatly improved the quality of its analysis.

At first, it was generally believed that the new process would greatly expand the power of Congress to shape budgets and concomitantly reduce the power of the President. In the summer of 1981, President Reagan showed, however, that with skillful public relations it was possible for a President to capture the process. He dominated the budget debate and was able successfully to implement a significant change in budget priorities. It is, in fact, doubtful that he would have been successful if the process had not existed because decision making would have then been drawn out over the year and less vulnerable to a sustained campaign on the part of the President.

It is too early to say whether the experiences of 1981 represented an aberration or whether we can expect Presidents to dominate the process periodically. But, whatever the answer to this question, I do believe that the process has made some important long-run contributions primarily because it has already served an important educational function. It has provided analysis and data, making the legislator, press, and public better informed regarding the relative importance of various budget issues. It should also be noted that it takes time for a new process to become well-established and for legislators to learn how to use it. I do believe, without being able to provide much evidence, that the process has the potential to become more effective in the future. It will, however, have to survive severe difficulties in the middle 1980s. The huge deficits created by the spending and tax legislation of 1981 have left Congress with no easy options. Their only choice is to cut programs and raise taxes. Politicians hate doing both, and since the relatively young process makes the unpleasant choices highly explicit, the process will not be popular, and it is always possible that it will be weakened.

PLANNING, PROGRAMING, BUDGETING SYSTEMS; MANAGEMENT BY OBJECTIVES; ZERO-BASE BUDGETING; AND SUNSET LAWS

Various Presidents since Lyndon Johnson have attempted to force more formal program evaluation on the bureaucracy. The goal is to provide information on the effectiveness of various programs so that decision makers and, through them, the voters can identify particularly wasteful government activities.

Planning, programing, and budgeting systems (PPBS) were used very effectively by Secretary of Defense Robert McNamara in the early 1960s to identify waste in the Pentagon. Impressed with his accomplishment, President Johnson attempted to impose the same techniques on the nondefense bureaucracy. The goal of the effort was to identify the benefits and costs of entire programs defined with reference to their goals, regardless of how their costs might be spread across several budget line items. It soon became apparent that the success of PPBS in the Pentagon presented more testimony to the extreme inefficiency which existed in that agency than it did to the effectiveness of the technique.

The application of the technique to social programs illustrated profound weaknesses in the approach. By their very nature, few products of government are traded on the marketplace. This makes it difficult to assess their value to the populace. Analysts use a variety of techniques to evaluate benefits, but typically the analysis must, by necessity, be based on fairly arbitrary assumptions. Because it is difficult to judge the validity of the assumptions, biased analysts can easily convert program evaluations into advocacy documents. In other words, program evaluation is as much an art as a science, and different "artists" will arrive at different interpretations. Theoretically, this problem could be reduced by forcing the production of competing evaluations from groups for and against the program, and decision makers and outside experts could make judgments about the quality and scientific basis of the various evaluations. But even one evaluation of each of the hundreds of federal programs generates mounds of paper, and President Johnson's system quickly suffered from information overload. It eventually collapsed under its own weight.

The Nixon administration responded by introducing management by objectives (MBO). Managers of the bureaucracy were to identify goals clearly—something that is seldom done in the legislation-creating programs—and to set out a schedule for meeting those goals. Program evaluation could be used to identify goals and costs. The Ford administration attempted to give program evaluation a more formal role in the system by insisting that cabinet secretaries select as objectives several programs each year for priority evaluations. This was an attempt to increase the use of program evaluation without swamping the system with paper as occurred under PPBS.

Managing the MBO system became almost as cumbersome as managing programs themselves. But the approach was initiated late in the Nixon administration, and the short duration of the Ford administration prevented it from getting a fair trial. It does have considerable appeal. Although it can be gamed by the bureaucracy who can set limited objectives, promulgate an easy schedule for meeting targets, and select only efficient programs for evaluation, an energetic President and White House staff can, in theory, limit the worst abuses. It does, however, require constant attention from the President, and this is difficult since he is constantly distracted by other matters, for example, in the foreign policy area. It is difficult to sustain his and the press's and public's attention to the problem of managing the bureaucracy. Compared to other issues, the problem of achieving good management seems totally without glamour.

President Carter, however, was able to make management efficiency a campaign issue in 1976. He promised to do wonders with zero-base budgeting (ZBB). Departments were forced to divide up programs into decision units. Objectives were to be defined for the units, and the implications of adding or reducing spending on the unit were to be evaluated. For each program, a minimum budget level at which the program could be effective was to be specified. Options for increasing spending above the minimum were then ranked along with options for reductions or for eliminating programs entirely. A budget restraint was then established and departments were to proceed down the ranking of options until their budget was enhanced.

The approach was as cumbersome as PPBS. Mountains of paper were generated, and a multitude of biased program evaluations poured forth. The system proved unworkable and was abandoned quietly.

Another approach toward inducing more careful program evaluation is the sunset law (SL). In this concept, all programs have a limited life. As their expiration date approaches, they are to be evaluated and are not supposed to be renewed unless they are proved to be effective. Although a number of sunset laws have been introduced in Congress, no comprehensive approach has ever passed. Several states have experimented with the approach, but results have been modest at best and nonexistent at worst. Although SL is not as cumbersome as PPBS or ZBB, it is still very demanding because of the large number of federal programs. Even a requirement that programs be assessed only periodically, say, every five years, probably generates more of a paperwork burden than can be handled effectively by the bureaucracy and Congress. Moreover, just as with PPBS and ZBB, the evaluations are likely to be advocacy documents rationalizing the continued existence of the program. The congressional committees who created the programs in the first place are unlikely to be very critical, and other decision makers are simply too busy to exercise oversight over the evaluation process.

In my own view, any comprehensive system that attempts to evaluate all government programs on a rigid schedule is unlikely to be effective. While program evaluations can play an important role in identifying inefficiency, our goals must be modest, and only a very few evaluations can be handled effectively each year.

A President working through the Office of Management and Budget can force departments to pick two or three programs for special attention each year. Cabinet secretaries must be warned that the President will not regard them kindly if they pick only their best programs for evaluation or if their analysis is slipshod and biased. But a system of this type requires constant attention by the President himself. The cabinet and bureaucracy will quickly assess the degree of interest of the President, and if he is not really interested in the management of the bureaucracy, no system will work.

CONSTITUTIONAL RESTRICTIONS

Many favor a constitutional amendment that would impose limits on the government's ability to run deficits and to raise tax burdens. Most variants directly or indirectly limit spending as well. The movement is based on two intellectual foundations. First, it is believed that the current system is biased toward more spending than is desired by the median voter. Second, it is believed that the Keynesian Revolution destroyed the justification for balancing the budget without replacing it with any other fiscal norm which would impose restraints on Congress. Therefore, it is believed that restraints must be put in the Constitution and most proposed constitutional amendments require some super-majority, say 60 percent, to approve a deficit.

While it is easy to sympathize with the arguments and goals of those proposing a constitutional amendment, it is hard to accept the notion that the approach would be workable. A loosely written amendment, which only stated goals or simply stated that Congress should plan for a balanced budget, would not be very effective. Budget totals are so dependent on economic forecasts that creative forecasting can almost always result in a planned budget balance. A more rigorous amendment which required a balanced budget or a certain tax burden on spending total as an outcome would be extremely difficult to administer. It could, in fact, do more harm than good.

There is, for example, a very high probability of legislative impasse in any system requiring a supermajority. Congress would often face a situation in which existing laws will lead to a deficit. It may be impossible either to get a majority vote to cut spending or raise taxes or to get a 60 percent vote to approve a deficit. Such an impasse could only be broken through logrolling, and since program spending is the currency used by politicians to buy votes and since purchasing a large deficit is as easy as purchasing a small deficit under all the proposed amendments, it is logically possible that spending and deficits would be larger than they would be if the amendment did not exist.

Another danger is that a rigid budget amendment would push politicians into achieving their goals by using regulations, government-sponsored institutions, and credit programs instead of using their taxing and spending powers. It is generally agreed that non-budget devices for commanding resources are less efficient and subject to even less control than are budget procedures. The whole government may become even less efficient as a result.

I believe that constitutional amendments that attempt to limit budget aggregates are misguided. If the Constitution is to be amended, I think that it would be more practical to give the President more power to limit spending. This could be accomplished by increasing presidential impoundment powers. Presumably, the President, who represents the entire nation, is less the victim of special-interest pressures than is the typical legislator, who represents a smaller, more specialized constituency. However, the Congress has traditionally been unwilling to sacrifice any of its own power and has been vehemently opposed to considering an impoundment amendment.

LIMITING SPENDING BY LIMITING TAX RECEIPTS

Economist Milton Friedman and others have argued that the best way to limit spending is to limit tax receipts. Economists Richard E. Wagner and James M. Buchanan have on the other side argued that deficits facilitate greater spending growth because the sale of bonds, being a voluntary exchange, represents a politically easy way to expand spending as opposed to levying compulsory taxes. The empirical evidence on the issue is murky, although the steady upward trend in deficits over the last two decades would seem to favor Wagner-Buchanan rather than Friedman. In any case, cutting taxes before cutting spending represents a risky strategy. The resulting deficits create huge policy uncertainty. It is not clear to private decision makers whether the deficits will be tolerated in the long run, whether they will be monetized, whether personal and/or business taxes will be raised, or whether they will be successful in limiting spending. Even if this technique works in the long run, it could do much short-term harm.

ACROSS-THE-BOARD CUTS IN SPENDING

It is sometimes proposed that all agencies should suffer equally during times of fiscal austerity. It is recognized that this approach is inefficient, but it is thought that by curbing everyone at once, the power of special-interest groups can be thwarted since they often coalesce to back each other's favorite spending programs when such programs are considered sequentially.

Unfortunately, this approach is simply not practical in the United States. Different agencies have different portions of their budgets tied up in long-run contractual commitments. For example, much of the budget of the Department of Housing and Urban Development (HUD) is dedicated to paying interest subsidies on thirty-year mortgages, whereas the Department of Justice has few commitments of this type. A 10 percent across-the-board cut would therefore mean that many of HUD's noncontractual programs would have to be cut by far more than 10 percent whereas Justice could handle such cuts more easily. In other words, an approach that, at first sight, appears to be even-handed is anything but. Adjusting for such differences becomes very complicated, and as soon as that happens the approach falls apart very quickly.

THE NEW FEDERALISM

President Reagan would like to place much more responsibility for nondefense programs at the state and local level. Cost-sharing grants for such programs would be initially replaced with block grants, and eventually federal assistance would be ended altogether.

It has been suggested earlier that a reduction in grants may have already played a role in slowing state and local spending. When states and localities have to raise the funds for programs themselves, it is reasonable to believe that the programs will be examined more critically. Decentralization could also be expected to reduce the power of special-interest groups. There are economies of scale in lobbying. Maintaining one office to influence federal legislation is a lot easier than maintaining fifty lobbies in various states.

It may be countered that the federal government has an interest in encouraging state and local activities that have beneficial impacts outside of their own geographical jurisdictions. This argument has merit, but it is hard to find evidence that the current federal grant system has been influenced much by a desire to maximize beneficial externalities subject to a budget restraint.

I see the New Federalism as a very promising technique for limiting total spending. It has the beneficial by-product of reducing the number of issues that have to be settled by federal legislators. It should allow them to specialize more on those issues that are truly federal and thus to make better informed decisions.

There are many inconsistencies in President Reagan's New Federalism proposal, e.g., some income redistribution programs such as aid to dependent children and food stamps are to be given to states and localities, while others such as medicaid are to be federalized. It is, therefore, unlikely to be adopted in its entirety. A more gradual movement toward decentralization is likely, and in fact there has been irregular movement in that direction ever since the Nixon administration adopted general revenue sharing. I see it as one of the most positive developments in the American political scene.

Social Security and Defense

The previous section described various techniques for controlling spending and most were found wanting. There were, however, a few glimmers of hope. A policy of selective program evaluation, vigorously supported by the President, can provide information that helps counter the biased data often produced by narrow-interest groups. The new congressional budget process has added to the rationality of congressional decision making and could make a more significant contribution in the future. Providing the President with stronger impoundment powers would also be helpful, and decentralizing decision making by devolving fiscal functions down to the state and local level would weaken the lobbyists and put the program decisions in the hands of those who are most directly influenced by program benefits and costs.

However, it is crucial to emphasize that none of these techniques is likely to reduce the relative burden of government significantly over the next decade unless they make some impact on two huge and rapidly growing functions of government which pose very special problems. Those functions are caring for the elderly and disabled and defending the country. Counting outlays on only the three main programs in the former category—Social Security, medicare, and supplementary security income—and adding them to defense outlays yields a spending total equal to 52 percent of the total outlays of fiscal 1981. If current spending policy is continued, these programs will constitute over 60 percent of total spending in fiscal 1987.

As already noted, the main political problem in contending with the elderly and disabled is the sheer size of the constituency. The constituency is not only large, it is extremely well-organized. It represents the most powerful lobbying group in the United States, and politicians live in abject fear of its power.

There is no shortage of efficient and equitable options for slowing the growth of the Social Security System, but it is hard to get a reasonable hearing. To cite but one example, almost all experts agree that some portion of Social Security benefits should be included in taxable income. Benefits are now tax free. But when the taxation of a portion of benefits was recommended by a recent presidential commission, a resolution opposing the recommendation was immediately introduced in the House of Representatives. Only one member of Congress voted against the resolution. None of the techniques discussed previously has a hope of being effective against such overwhelmingly powerful political forces.

It is not easy to be optimistic about our prospects for dealing with this situation. As I see it, the only hope lies in convincing the constituency itself that by blocking reasonable reforms, they are in danger of killing the taxpayer goose that is laying their golden eggs.

The possibility of dampening the demands of the elderly is not quite as preposterous as it sounds. First, it is necessary to emphasize that there is no need to reduce the real benefits of those already retired. The big problem involves the rise in real average benefits for each successful cohort of retirees that is promised by current law. Slowing that rise by even one-half of one percentage point per year could save massive amounts of money in the long run. Second, convincing the elderly of the need for a reduced rate of growth of real benefits will become easier as the elderly become better off. As recently as the early 1960s, the elderly as a group were among the poorest groups in American society. Since that time their economic status has improved more rapidly than that of any other group, and, if in-kind benefits are counted, the incidence of poverty among the elderly is now lower than that in the population as a whole. Since the middle 1970s, the relative improvement in the status of the elderly has been especially rapid, primarily because real wage rates have fallen in the rest of the economy.

I do not want to seem overly optimistic about convincing the elderly to dampen their demands, but they should at least become less frantic about protecting their benefits as their economic status improves. Recent attempts to curb the Social Security System's growth may have failed miserably, but it is significant to note that options for slowing benefit growth are now being debated openly by politicians. They may not yet be ready to vote for reform, but ten years ago the issue could not even be raised in public. The only issue open to debate was how fast to expand the system.

The problem of enhancing the efficiency of defense spending is easier to handle politically, but very difficult to analyze conceptually. Much spending is directed at protecting ourselves from events that have a tiny probability of occurring but which would have disastrous consequences if they did emerge. The question "How much is enough?" is not easy to answer when we are discussing the survival of a nation.

While there is a fairly broad consensus among Social Security experts regarding the efficiency and equity implications of various options that would slow the growth of Social Security benefits, there seems to be less consensus among defense experts regarding the worth of complex, highly expensive systems such as the MX missile, the B-1 bomber, and nuclear carrier task forces. The sinking of British war ships in the Falklands is now being used as evidence that (a) large ships are obsolete or (b) only task forces centered by large carriers can protect themselves against missile attacks.

How can the nonexpert legislator or voter decide who is right? They probably cannot. However, military spending like all other spending should be rationed. Currently, the U.S. military is having virtually every wish fulfilled. It may be necessary to impose rationing using very crude rules of thumb.

Although it is totally unsatisfactory intellectually, the issue tends to be debated using the crudest possible quantitative criterion. Should real defense spending grow at 7 percent per year between now and 1987 or 5 percent? Should the United States devote 6 percent of the GNP to defense or 8 percent?

Note that all of these numbers imply a much larger U.S. defense effort than occurred during the last decade. There is a broad consensus favoring that course. The debate is only about how much greater the effort should be.

It may not be possible to improve the quality of the debate very much beyond using crude aggregate rules of thumb. However, I would make one strong suggestion. It was noted earlier that PPBS techniques were effectively applied in the Pentagon in the early 1960s. After years of financial stringency, it is probably safe to say that the Pentagon of the 1980s is more efficient than that of the 1950s. But there is still a need to enhance the intensity and quality of program analysis. The Reagan administration has been moving in the opposite direction. The role of program analysis has been downgraded because program analysts are disliked by the military professionals who are now in the ascendancy. There is room for reversing past trends by placing somewhat more emphasis on analysis. In the long run, such a reform should serve the interest of those wanting a stronger defense. Politicians who oppose the military will be constantly searching for examples of extreme waste, and with the current U.S. defense program such examples will be easy to find. There is a danger that examples of waste will provoke a public reaction that will cause the pendulum of public opinion to swing in a vehemently antimilitary direction. Obviously, better program analysis cannot prevent waste entirely, but it can reduce the probability of fiascos. It is, therefore, my strong conclusion that while reducing the power of the analysts may serve the short-run interests of the Reagan administration, it represents a grave error relative to their long-run interests.

Conclusions

The analysis of this chapter has not been very reassuring. It has primarily been about techniques that have not worked in the past or are unlikely to work in the future. Yet, there are glimmers of hope. Decentralization of decision making to state and local levels appears promising. The congressional budget process shows signs of becoming more and more effective if it can survive the extreme pressures of the next few years. A President who gives high priority to better management can have an impact on the bureaucracy, and intensified program analysis in the Pentagon may lead to more effective military spending.

But the overwhelming conclusion is that better budget control is not easy to obtain. It is an arduous step-by-step process requiring much effort. It will not be obtained by simple-minded blunderbuss techniques. Devices such as the constitutional amendments are only likely to complicate the decision making with no real results. The one rule with certain validity is to beware of politicians bearing simple solutions.

Benjamin M. Friedman

4

Monetary Policy Management

Introduction

The decade of the 1970s marked a period of great transition for the conduct of monetary policy in the United States, just as for the U.S. economy as a whole. Since 1970 the economic setting confronting U.S. monetary policy has changed, and with it the role that the economy needs monetary policy to play. In response, by the beginning of the late 1980s the Federal Reserve System formulated and implemented monetary policy far differently than it did ten years earlier.

Even so, there is reason to believe that this transition is not yet complete. As always, of course, uncertainties remain, and the economic setting will no doubt evolve still further. Perhaps more importantly, the pattern of conduct of monetary policy adopted during the 1970s not only fails to deal with several important

BENJAMIN M. FRIEDMAN *is professor of economics at Harvard University and director of financial markets and monetary economics research at the National Bureau of Economic Research. Previously, Dr. Friedman worked at Morgan Stanley & Co., an investment banking firm, and also worked in consulting or other capacities with the board of governors of the Federal Reserve System, as well as the Federal Reserve Banks of both New York and Boston. Author of* Monetary Policy in the United States *and editor of* The Changing Roles of Debt and Equity in Financing U.S. Capital Formation, *among other books, he has also written numerous articles on other aspects of economic policy.*

aspects of macroeconomic management but also, even taken on its own terms, suffers from significant shortcomings. Correcting those shortcomings and, if possible, addressing further macro-economic issues of broader dimension constitute the structural challenge confronting U.S. monetary policy in the 1980s.

The changes that took place in both the setting and the conduct of U.S. monetary policy during the 1970s were profound and far-reaching. Perhaps most importantly, as *price inflation* accelerated and became more volatile, the balance of opinion turned toward emphasizing the promotion of price stability as the chief objective of monetary policy. Full utilization of the economy's labor and capital resources remained a major concern, to be sure. By the end of the decade, however, the price stability goal had clearly taken precedence over the full-employment goal for monetary policy purposes. (The same was not, and today is not, true of fiscal policy, however—more on this below.)

This single most significant change in the economic setting in turn led fairly directly to the first major change that took place during this period in the actual conduct of monetary policy. Before 1970 the Federal Reserve System had typically conducted monetary policy by choosing and then setting a short-term market rate of interest—for example, the federal funds rate (or, equivalently, the net free reserve position of the banking system). As people became more anxious about regaining price stability, however, they attached more importance to the connection between the economy's rate of price inflation and its rate of money growth. At the same time, they also gradually became aware of the increased difficulty of judging the economic implications of any given observed (nominal) interest rate level in an inflationary environment. During the early 1970s, therefore, the Federal Reserve System changed its policy framework to focus on targeted growth rates for selected monetary aggregates, although it still relied on setting a short-term interest rate as the means of achieving its monetary targets. Then, in October 1979, it abandoned its concern for interest rates altogether and adopted a new monetary targeting procedure based on setting the growth of bank reserves. If the advent of price inflation and the desire for price stability were the only changes in the underlying economic environment, the transition in the formulation and implementation of monetary policy would perhaps be complete with these two changes made in the 1970s.

Inflation and discontent with inflation are not the only new factors, however. At least two further new aspects of the setting confronting monetary policy are less favorable to the major changes in the policy framework adopted in the 1970s. In large part because of them, the transition in U.S. monetary policy is probably not complete. The adoption first of the monetary targets strategy and then of the reserves operating procedure is not likely to be—indeed, ought not to be—the end of the story.

The most obvious other new factor in the underlying setting is the greatly accelerated pace of *financial innovation*. Innovation has often been easier in the financial industry than in other lines of business, but since 1970 the explosion of new instruments, new institutions, and new ways of using old ones has outstripped any recent experience. More importantly, many of the financial innovations of the 1970s have directly impaired the usefulness of a monetary policy strategy based on target rates of growth for specific monetary aggregates.

Yet an additional new factor in this setting, familiar enough in other contexts but too little discussed in connection with monetary policy, is the newly discovered vulnerability of the U.S. economy to *supply-side "shocks."* After the experience of the 1970s, including oil and other foreign-source supply shocks, as well as domestic-source shocks to agricultural prices and industrial productivity, it is no longer plausible to proceed under the old presumption that the U.S. economy would grow smoothly through time were it not for occasional disturbances to aggregate demand. Supply shocks matter too, and at times they matter more than demand shocks. In the presence of supply shocks, however, there is no reason to believe that simply stabilizing the money growth rate constitutes a desirable monetary policy.

Hence the transition in U.S. monetary policy is not complete. There is more work to be done in adapting the nation's monetary policy framework even to those changes in the underlying economic setting that have already taken place—not to mention whatever further adaptation the economy's future evolution will require. A major goal of thoughtful discourse about monetary policy today should, therefore, be to find ways of narrowing the gap between the policy framework now in place and the requirements of the economy in the 1980s.

The object of this chapter is to work toward that goal at two levels. First, the chapter considers a pair of broad issues defining the role that U.S. monetary policy should play as one part of a more comprehensive system of macroeconomic management. Here the chief problems are to understand what is plausible to ask of macroeconomic policy in general and to determine how monetary policy should fit into this wider system. The chapter then goes on to consider, from the narrower perspective of monetary policy alone, how the Federal Reserve System should formulate and implement monetary policy so as best to enable it to play this role. Here the chief problems are to draw a balance of some objectives against others and to evaluate—on largely empirical grounds, since few genuinely useful conclusions on these questions are available on the basis of logical argument alone—the relative merits of alternative operating procedures. The chapter concludes by briefly summarizing the major lessons drawn for monetary policy.

The Role of Monetary Policy in Macroeconomic Management

The goals of macroeconomic management in almost every advanced, industrialized economy have traditionally included price stability, economic growth, full employment, and international balance. Even in economies (or at times) in which economic policy makers have ignored one or more of these objectives, their doing so has typically reflected the belief that policy actions could not affect the omitted objective, rather than lack of regard for the objective itself.

It is a commonplace that the most interesting problems confronting macroeconomic management arise from mutual inconsistencies (except perhaps in the very long run) among the major policy objectives to be pursued. Even so, at a fundamental level, policy choices do not always reduce to a simple matter of value judgments. Some policy-making frameworks are more likely to promote widely agreed upon objectives than are others. Conversely, some policy frameworks render the economy more vulnerable to risks—of inflation, of instability in business activity, of financial rupture, and so on—than do others.

In charting the best way to seek these familiar objectives, it is necessary first of all to have some idea of what is plausible to ask macroeconomic management to deliver. The insistence upon unrealistic goals may easily lead to a poorly functioning policy framework. Then, given a sense of what is feasible, the next step is to resolve the respective roles associated with the major instruments of macroeconomic policy, including especially monetary and fiscal policy.

FEASIBLE OBJECTIVES FOR MONETARY POLICY

The economic dilemma confronting the United States in the 1980s is to reverse two sharply adverse developments that set in much earlier on in the post–World War II period. Price inflation has gradually accelerated from close to zero in the early 1960s to close to 10 percent two decades later, with significant breaks only during sharply punctuated episodes associated with business downturns. At the same time, productivity growth began to slow by the late 1960s and then suffered more sharply throughout the next decade. Not only was each of these developments taken on its own undesirable, but also their confluence was especially unfortunate in that conventional policy prescriptions aimed at dealing with either apparently had still further adverse consequences for the other.

The problem posed for macroeconomic policy was, and is, to resolve this dilemma. Economists have responded to this challenge in several ways, but the most optimistic response—and, not coincidentally, that which has gained the most attention and tentative acceptance in political circles—has been to sever the dilemma by arguing that it is, after all, possible to consider each of its two components separately. Price inflation, according to this logic, is simply a monetary phenomenon to be cured by an appropriate monetary policy involving a slower rate of money growth. Further, slower money growth (especially if advertised well in advance, on some accounts) need not adversely affect real economic activity in general or business capital formation (and hence productivity) in particular. Similarly, business capital formation, according to the companion logic, is simply a fiscal phenomenon to be cured by an appropriate fiscal policy involving lower marginal tax rates (especially on returns to saving and investment). Further, the government budget deficits resulting from these tax reductions need not adversely affect either the ability of the Federal Reserve System to implement an antiinflationary monetary policy or the ability of the economy's private business sector to finance net new investment in productive plant and equipment. Hence monetary policy and fiscal policy, acting entirely independently, can pursue separate respective goals and thereby solve the dilemma. To a first approximation, this approach has been the one actually pursued in the United States at the outset of the 1980s.

The time has now come (it actually arrived some time ago) to recognize that this bifurcated approach to the nation's macro-economic dilemma is artificial in conception and counterproductive in practice. Slower monetary growth does *not* slow inflation without costs measured by foregone output and incomes and by a poorer environment for business capital formation. Fiscal incentives do *not* increase saving and investment in a very straightforward or immediate way, especially if business activity is stagnant or shrinking. Reductions in tax rates do *not* raise tax revenues in any short or intermediate run, and the resulting deficits do affect conditions for financing business investment. In short, monetary and fiscal policies can *not* pursue their respective goals independently.

The first important conclusion for monetary policy, then, is that it is not plausible to expect a costless disinflation. Reversing the trend of two decades toward ever more rapid inflation has already, and will later on, involve substantial costs. Indeed, these costs are just the real economic processes by which monetary policy slows inflation in the first place. Moreover, these costs do not accrue solely to low-income workers whom the rest of the body politic is usually prepared to sacrifice in the name of one worthy cause or another. The costs of disinflation accrue to business (and, through corporate ownership, to all shareholders) as well as to labor. In addition, reductions in business net capital formation as a result of either a weak economy or a stringent financing environment, both of which typically follow from an antiinflationary monetary policy, impose costs on the entire economy in the form of foregone future gains in productivity and, hence, general living standards.

Monetary policy *can* reduce inflation, but not without cost. Giving up the illusion that monetary policy can achieve costless disinflation is an important first step in considering appropriate macroeconomic policies. If monetary policy is to assume a genuinely antiinflationary stance until the improvement in price stability becomes more than a temporary cyclical break, it will be necessary to forego other desirable objectives.

Can monetary policy also promote net capital formation? Here the answer differs according to short versus long time horizons and according to direct versus indirect effects associated with monetary policy. During the course of a disinflation, for example, tight monetary policy presumably depresses investment directly by raising the (real) cost of, and reducing the availability of, financing. Indeed, the direct effects associated with monetary policy can either boost or retard the economy's investment performance for periods of several years at a time. Over longer periods, however, there is little evidence that monetary policy can importantly affect real (that is, after-inflation) interest rates on an ongoing basis and, hence, little reason to believe that monetary policy can *directly* affect investment.

By contrast, even on an ongoing basis, monetary policy appears to affect *indirectly* both the amount and the composition of the economy's physical capital formation, by either fostering or impairing the smooth functioning of the economy's markets for financial capital. For example, the Federal Reserve System's choice of operating procedures for monetary policy in part determines the volatility of interest rates and financial asset prices more generally (more on this below). This volatility in turn affects the risk premium required by investors holding assets and, hence, imposed on businesses issuing liabilities (or equities) to finance new plant and equipment. In addition, interest rate volatility also plays a large role in determining the probability of bankruptcy for any given enterprise and, hence, affects risk premiums on private securities in yet another way. Once again, a monetary policy that promotes stability in interest rates and asset prices and, hence, minimizes bankruptcy risks also helps to promote capital formation.

In sum, it is implausible to seek a monetary policy that will achieve costless disinflation, and a negative impact on capital formation is one part of the cost of an antiinflationary monetary policy. At the same time, in a long-run context the contribution of monetary policy to the promotion of capital formation is probably limited to the fostering of smoothly functioning financial markets, without the volatility that raises risk premiums for all classes of borrowers and especially for private business borrowing.

COORDINATING MONETARY AND FISCAL POLICIES

The fact that monetary and fiscal policies do not simply affect separate aspects of the economy's performance without implication for one another's effectiveness immediately raises the issue of monetary-fiscal coordination. As the discussion above has already indicated, the most important context in which potential inconsistencies between these two policies arise in the early 1980s is the prospect of an antiinflationary monetary policy's impeding the enhanced capital formation sought by fiscal policy, while a deficit-prone fiscal policy complicates (or, in the extreme, precludes) the implementation of an antiinflationary monetary policy in the first place. As the 1981–1982 business recession dragged to an end, the issue in even more specific terms was whether the U.S. economy would or would not stage a vigorous postrecession recovery of traditional dimension. Even apart from any specific context, however, the simultaneous pursuits of intertwined goals by interrelated policy instruments ·clearly raises the need for some coordination between them.

The political independence of the Federal Reserve System, traditionally a hallowed aspect of the time-honored art of central banking as practiced in the United States, has recently attracted increasing scrutiny and even outright criticism. As not only economic theorists but also the general public have become increasingly aware of the power of monetary policy to affect the nation's economy for good or ill, many thoughtful people have questioned the institutional structure which delegates this power to a quasi-judicial body. The ongoing economic policy tug of war between successive Republican administrations and Democratic-controlled Congresses has further highlighted the political aspects of the Federal Reserve System's independent ability to throw the weight of monetary policy toward stimulating or restraining business activity.

The Federal Reserve Act, passed by Congress in 1913, created as the nation's central bank a Federal Reserve System consisting of an appointed board of governors in Washington and twelve regional Federal Reserve Banks, each having its own board of directors made up of private citizens. With respect to authority over the tools of monetary policy, the Federal Reserve Board fixes the reserve requirements which member banks must hold against deposits, while the regional boards of directors (acting subject to approval by the Federal Reserve Board) fix the discount rate at which member banks may borrow from their respective Federal Reserve Banks.

In practice, however, the most important monetary policy tool is open market operations—that is, the purchase and sale of securities directly for the account of the Federal Reserve System—which were not even contemplated in 1913. Consequently, the mechanism for exercising this means of economic control had to evolve in response to the gradual realization during the 1920s of what open market operations were and how and why they worked. The establishment of the Federal Open Market Committee, a body of twelve (consisting of the seven members of the board of governors plus five of the twelve presidents of the regional Federal Reserve Banks) centralized decision-making authority over open market operations. By doing so, it determined the trend toward ever increasing centralization of power over virtually all aspects of monetary policy in the Federal Reserve Board and, in particular, in its chairman. The use of open market operations for macroeconomic policy purposes finally came into its own in 1951, when the Treasury–Federal Reserve Accord relieved the Federal Reserve System of its wartime obligation to support the prices of (that is, hold down the yields on) long-term U.S. government securities. Open market operations have remained the centerpiece of monetary policy ever since.

The Federal Reserve System has recently received much attention from many quarters and substantial criticism from most. Typically, a major issue is the apparent independence with which it determines monetary policy. The members of the board of governors are presidential appointees confirmed by the Senate, but their fourteen-year terms of office provide insulation against the more immediate pressures of partisan politics. Also at the appointment of the President, and with the confirmation of the Senate, one member serves a four-year term in the chairmanship—a position of increasingly great personal power and visibility. The regional presidents, who form a sizable minority of the key Federal Open Market Committee, are selected by the boards of directors of their respective Federal Reserve Banks without any necessary formal presidential or congressional approval.

While this degree of independence is somewhat familiar among the vast array of federal regulatory agencies, the Federal Reserve System's responsibilities extend beyond those typically granted to a specific regulatory commission. As the sole agency responsible for formulating and implementing monetary policy, the Federal Reserve System's macroeconomic policy role is almost coequal with Congress's control over fiscal policy, and even the latter is subject to presidential veto. Especially in a climate of relative disillusionment with the capacity of fiscal policy and enthusiasm for that of monetary policy, the system's unfettered control over monetary policy sometimes seems to many observers to be the single most important influence on the course of the U.S. economy. Indeed, while most economists believe that the time lags with which monetary policy influences business activity are longer than the corresponding fiscal policy lags, critics of the Federal Reserve System's independence argue that its compact decision structure in fact gives it the ability to counter or even anticipate fiscal policy decisions produced by the cumbersome congresssional committee process. With a committee of twelve meeting privately once per month, and able to shift the direction of monetary policy at any meeting, the Federal Reserve System has the advantage of traveling light.

What is the best way to coordinate monetary and fiscal policies in light of this arrangement? The principles of a democratic republic seem to indicate that Congress and the President have the authority, and indeed the responsibility, to determine the nation's broad macroeconomic objectives. They should, of course, receive the advice of the Federal Reserve System on questions of what goals are feasible and what implications arise from pursuing any particular feasible path; but, in case of a conflict between the objectives preferred by the central bank and those chosen by Congress and the President, the central bank must defer. The Federal Reserve System must use monetary policy to pursue the broad economic objectives specified by Congress and the President, not to offset fiscal policy actions aimed at effecting these targets. Indeed, the Constitution makes clear that in the first instance Congress is responsible for monetary policy, so that the Federal Reserve System exercises this power by delegation from Congress. For the same reasons, the specific policy mix to use in pursuit of this set of macroeconomic objectives must ultimately be the decision of Congress and the President. The Federal Reserve System should not be able to force fiscal policy to shift course by resolutely holding to a monetary policy at odds with the policy mix selected by Congress and the President. At this level, however, the advice of the Federal Reserve System should be an especially important input to the decision-making process, since it is presumably best equipped, among the elements of the federal government, to assess the potential impacts of monetary policy actions.

Finally, at the level of specific actions for implementing monetary policy in its selected role, the importance of the Federal Reserve System's own expertise seems to outweigh other considerations. While periodic assessment of the success or failure of policy actions after the fact is always useful—and the congressional oversight process formalized under the Humphrey-Hawkins Act of 1978 is important in this regard—continuous interference with the Federal Reserve System's ongoing operations can only be counterproductive.

These considerations notwithstanding, there is now no mechanism for Congress and the President to agree on basic macroeconomic goals. The "Economic Report of the President" and the annual budget proposal submitted by the administration in principle constitute one assessment, although the realism of these documents' projections has increasingly come under question. Decisions reached by the congressional budget committees represent an alternative statement, but these resolutions too have their drawbacks. What is needed is a combined statement passed by Congress and accepted by the President. Moreover, even if such a combined statement of realistic objectives existed, there is now no coherent mechanism for Congress and the President (not to mention the Federal Reserve System) to determine the best macroeconomic policy mix for achieving these targets.

Part of this problem, of course, stems from the give-and-take nature of the congressional decision process. Who can speak for Congress about its macroeconomic objectives, or even its plans for fiscal policy? The congressional budget committees are an uncertain step in the direction of centralizing at least some aspects of Congress's thinking about the implications of the expenditure side of fiscal policy actions, and the House Ways and Means Committee and the Senate Finance Committee have similar dominance on tax matters. Nevertheless, final decision authority still rests with the full House and Senate, and anticipating the outcome of taxing or spending decisions remains difficult at best.

Another part of the problem is a product of the presidential system of government itself, especially when the administration in office does not enjoy the support of a clear majority in Congress. Even if it is plain that the tide of opinion in Congress favors a particular set of policy objectives and a particular policy mix, is there sufficient unanimity to override a potential presidential veto? What monetary policy actions is the Federal Reserve System to adopt if the President and the congressional majority differ sharply over fundamental macroeconomic choices?

The problem is yet further complicated by the tendency among both the President and Congress to blur the distinction between what is desirable and what is feasible. Official statements about the planned path of the economy are typically skewed toward optimism. Still, judging good faith efforts at setting realistic objectives is far from straightforward, because differences over what is desired so often go in tandem with honest disagreements over what is feasible.

Even at the level of specific central bank actions to implement the role of monetary policy in the selected overall policy mix, a matter best left to the discretion of the Federal Reserve System, it may well be difficult to distinguish between the Federal Reserve System's monetary policy responsibility and its regulatory responsibilities for financial markets. The interdependence of these two functions can create conflicts in which some of its actions—for example, large loans to threatened banks—would appear counter to the selected overall thrust of monetary policy.

In light of all these impediments, monetary-fiscal coordination is likely to remain a matter best handled—as now—by informal consultations among officials of Congress, the administration, and the Federal Reserve System. Even so, there is at least one formal step which, if taken, could significantly enhance prospects for better coordination. In particular Congress should require the Federal Reserve System, as part of the chairman's semiannual reports under the Humphrey-Hawkins Act of 1978, to state precisely the set of basic macroeconomic policy objectives at which the Federal Reserve System is aiming in its current monetary policy stance. (The current system of reporting ranges spanning individual Federal Open Market Committee's members' views is simply not adequate.) Requiring the Federal Reserve System to state its basic macroeconomic objectives would probably be sufficient to ensure that the thrust of monetary policy lies within the scope of whatever consensus existed between Congress and the President. Given the ever present possibility of amending the Federal Reserve Act of 1913, political realities already render monetary policy less independent in practice than it may be in theory anyway, and this disclosure requirement would further guarantee that the conduct of monetary policy not be inconsistent with the political principles of a democratic republic.

Formulating and Implementing Monetary Policy

Once the political process has determined what role monetary policy should play in the overall structure of macroeconomic management at any time, it remains for the Federal Reserve System to execute monetary policy accordingly. Although the specifics of such decisions (for example, faster or slower targeted money growth at any time or higher or lower interest rates) are what usually attract attention, the more fundamental issue is the choice of the underlying framework that systematically governs the formulation and implementation of monetary policy. Especially since the Federal Reserve System has often instituted major changes in its monetary policy framework, including twice during the

1970s, there is no reason to regard such more basic issues as permanently settled. In addition, both the rapid pace of financial innovation and the prevalence of shocks to the economy's supply side since 1970 suggest that this framework as it exists today is not the best available basis for conducting monetary policy in the 1980s.

Because the Federal Reserve System currently uses an "intermediate target" system to conduct monetary policy, as do the central banks of most other industrialized non-Communist countries, it is helpful to consider the choice of monetary policy framework by first asking whether intermediate targets provide a sound basis for this purpose. To the extent that monetary policy will continue to rely on intermediate targets (for either economic or political reasons), two questions then arise: what should the intermediate targets be, and what operating procedure should the Federal Reserve System use to achieve these targets?

THE INTERMEDIATE TARGET STRATEGY

Central banks have often found it useful to formulate and implement monetary policy by focusing on some intermediate target or targets. Under an intermediate target strategy, the central bank specifies some financial variable(s)—in the United States since 1970, the major monetary aggregates—to stand as proxy for the real economic objectives at which monetary policy ultimately aims, such as economic growth and price stability. The result is, in effect, a two-step procedure. The central bank first determines what growth of the intermediate target is most likely to correspond to the desired ultimate economic outcome. It then sets some operating instrument over which it can exert close control —in the United States either a short-term interest rate or, since October 1979, the quantity of reserves—so as to achieve that growth rate for the intermediate target itself.

The essence of the intermediate target strategy is that, under it, the central bank is required to respond quickly and fully to any information reflected in the movements of whatever the intermediate target happens to be. Under the current framework in the United States, with monetary aggregates used as the intermediate targets, any movement in the public's money holdings immediately creates a presumption that the Federal Reserve System should react. In principle the Federal Reserve System is always free to change the money growth targets, of course, but in practice it is typically reluctant to do so. The intermediate target strategy instead calls for actions aimed at regaining the stated targets, so that the economic signals contained in movements of the monetary aggregates create a presumption of immediate response. By contrast, the presumption of this strategy, strictly implemented, is that there will be no response to signals arising from other sources but not reflected in the intermediate targets.

This strategy clearly makes sense only if movements of the intermediate targets bear some close and reliable relationship to the nonfinancial objectives of macroeconomic policy (more on this below). Indeed, just this line of reasoning was important in the adoption of the monetary aggregates as intermediate targets in the first place. At least from the perspective of the underlying financial environment, the key development that led the Federal Reserve System to abandon the setting of short-term interest rates, its basic approach to monetary policy as of the late 1960s, was probably the emergence in the U.S. economy of rapid and volatile price inflation. Once the new inflationary environment took hold in the financial markets, the problems inherent in basing monetary policy on nominal interest rates became apparent.

Although there are a number of reasons why nominal interest rates per se affect many kinds of activity in the U.S. economy (for example, the effect of deposit interest ceilings), most of the logic that suggests a connection between interest rates and nonfinancial economic activity more appropriately refers to real interest rates— that is, the nominal interest rates observed in the market, adjusted for borrowers' and lenders' expectations about inflation. In an era of high and volatile inflation rates, performing this adjustment appeared to be just too difficult. Moreover, the interaction between inflation and the tax code complicates the matter still further, since borrowers can deduct from taxable income the part of their nominal interest payments which serves to compensate lenders for the erosion in value of their outstanding principal, while at the same time most lenders pay tax on this premium.

As the awareness of inflation and its effects became more widespread, therefore, interest rates became less useful as a focus for monetary policy. By contrast, a monetary policy based on the growth of the money stock—an idea that some economists had proposed for a long time—appeared to be unaffected by this new development. The Federal Reserve System adopted the monetary targets framework in the early 1970s, and the "Ms" have occupied center stage in the design and execution of U.S. monetary policy ever since.

Changes in the financial environment, of course, were hardly the only reason underlying the adoption of the monetary targets framework. As the discussion above has already emphasized, the increasing focus on price inflation itself as a major economic policy problem, together with the belief that the rate of money growth placed an effective ceiling on the economy's inflation rate, was an important factor in this development. So too was the belief (at that time) among many economists that the supply side of the U.S. economy was essentially stable and that economic fluctuations were due mostly to instability in aggregate demand which a more stable money growth rate could help avoid. Finally, a matter of importance, at least to economists, was the belief that behavior in the economy's financial markets, including especially decisions by households and businesses about how much money to hold, was more dependably stable than were important aspects of behavior in the economy's product and factor markets.

Now, however, financial innovation (among other factors at work) has led to developments that have severely impaired the usefulness of the monetary targets approach. In response to changes in economic conditions, changes in competitive pressures, changes in available technologies (especially for communications and data processing), and changes in government regulations, financial market participants have introduced a wave of new financial instruments and new ways of using old ones. The immediate implication of these innovations—including NOW accounts, sweep accounts, money market mutual funds, money market certificates, repurchase agreements, and so on—is that measuring "money" has become anything but straightforward. Acting in response to these developments, the Federal Reserve Board in 1980 undertook a major redefinition of the major monetary aggregates, in effect abolishing the traditional "M1" and "M2" measures that an entire generation of economists had studied. Further, less sweeping redefinitions of the new Ms have subsequently occurred on an irregular basis. Nevertheless, it still remains unclear just what economic meaning to associate with any specific set of assets grouped together and defined as "money."

These same changes in the financial environment have also called into question some of the other key presumptions underlying the adoption of the monetary targets framework. The historical money demand relationship all but collapsed in its conventional form in the mid–1970s. Subsequent research emphasizing the effects of financial innovations on the demand for money has discovered new relationships that fit the historical data better, but there is little ground for confidence in the face of potential further changes. Similarly, the relationship between the inflation rate and the growth rate of any particular monetary aggregate is now more difficult to pin down. Meanwhile, oil shocks and agricultural price shocks during this same period have powerfully illustrated the importance of instability on the economy's supply side as a cause of economic fluctuations.

For all of these reasons, today's disillusionment with the monetary targets framework now underlying U.S. monetary policy is not simply a matter of unhappiness over the economy's recent performance. After all, any specific adverse economic experience could be due to either poor policy decisions, poor execution, or even bad luck rather than an inadequate framework. The desire for change today is instead more fundamental and, therefore, more persuasive. The well-understood propositions that would favor the exclusive reliance on monetary aggregate targets, if they were true, just do not match today's environment.

If the intermediate target strategy with the monetary aggregates as the central targets is faulty, what should the Federal Reserve System do in its place? One plausible response to these changed circumstances would be to reject the usefulness of any intermediate target at all for monetary policy. Without an intermediate target, the Federal Reserve System would focus its policy directly on the nonfinancial economy—which, after all, constitutes the ultimate reason for having a monetary policy. For example, some economists have argued that the Federal Reserve System should directly target the growth rate of nominal gross national product. Although the desirability of a single nominal income target is

questionable, in general a direct approach, without the intervention of any intermediate target between monetary policy actions
and desired nonfinancial outcomes, would constitute the most
effective policy framework on purely economic grounds.

Primarily for reasons that are more political than economic
in any narrow sense, however, both Congress and even the Federal
Reserve System itself appear firmly committed, at least for the
immediate future, to having some kind of intermediate target to
facilitate monitoring monetary policy on an ongoing basis. The
main reason goes, once again, to the question of how to conduct an
"independent" monetary policy in a democratic republic. If the
Federal Reserve System simply reported to Congress a target for
nominal income growth, for example, there would be no straightforward way to determine after the fact whether a failure to meet
this target reflected an inappropriate monetary policy, an inconsistent fiscal policy, unexpected oil or other supply shocks,
or still other relevant factors. In order to provide at least some
accountability of monetary policy—accountability in the political
sense, that is—it is necessary to move the discussion of monetary
policy to a point in the economic process closer to the source.
Intermediate targets, whatever their other failings, do just that.
The central factor dictating their use today is probably the desire to provide at least some form of accountability of monetary
policy in this sense.

If the desire for monetary policy accountability does lead
Congress to continue to require, and the Federal Reserve System
to continue to use, an intermediate target strategy, a major problem is likely to be continued financial innovation. Here consideration of the innovations of the 1970s does suggest two lessons for
the design of a framework for implementing monetary policy in
the 1980s. First, the effect of financial innovations on the economic
relationships that matter for monetary policy is often quite local-
ized. Specific instruments become either more or less attractive,
and specific aggregates consequently gain or lose importance without major consequences for many other aggregates. The chief implication of this lesson is that *diversification,* in the sense of relying
on disparate sources of signals, is likely to be superior to exclusive
reliance on any one source. Second, the evidence for substitution
within financial portfolios is substantially stronger than any evi-

dence found to date on financial-nonfinancial substitutions. Hence a sharp movement of portfolios into some new (or newly attractive) instrument is very likely to be associated with a movement out of something else. The chief implication of this lesson is that *broader aggregates,* which internalize many such shifts, are likely to be superior to narrow ones.

Within these broad guidelines, the choice of a monetary policy framework for the 1980s is a more open issue today than has been true for quite a few years. As people have continued to examine closely the course of monetary policy and its impact on economic events, they have increasingly begun to question not only the specific stance of monetary policy at any time but also the underlying framework that defines monetary policy at the basic decision-making level. Some students of the subject have advocated a focus on new targets, some have advocated retention of the old ones, and some have advocated abolition of any explicit targets whatsoever. The range of choice is unusually broad, and the issue is of paramount importance.

CHOOSING AN INTERMEDIATE TARGET

The structure of the intermediate target system suggests four important criteria for choosing a suitable target. First and most obviously, the target should be closely and reliably related to the nonfinancial objectives of monetary policy. Despite the proven seductiveness of discussions about whether any given M will or will not be within the announced target range, it is important never to lose sight of the simple truth that any such aggregate has no policy significance in and of itself. What matters is the effect of monetary policy on the nonfinancial economy, and intermediate targets not reliably related to that effect have no role at all to play in the monetary policy process.

Second, the relationship between the intermediate target and nonfinancial economic activity should be more than that of a mirror providing a reflection. For example, targeting a financial aggregate that just moved in step with nominal income, without affecting the subsequent movement of nominal income, would provide no advantages over directly targeting nominal income itself. Instead, movements of the intermediate target should contain information about the future movements of the nonfinancial objectives of monetary policy.

Third, the intermediate target should be closely and reliably related not only to the nonfinancial objectives of policy but also to the operating instruments that the central bank can control directly—in the U.S. context, once again, either reserves or a short-term interest rate. For example, although common stock prices in the United States are a well-known leading indicator of business activity, there is little evidence to suggest that the Federal Reserve System could exert sufficiently close control over the stock market to make it a good monetary policy target. There would be little point in having an intermediate target that the central bank could not expect to affect reasonably closely within some plausible time horizon determined by considerations of what matters for the economy as well as what provides political accountability.

Fourth, at the most practical level, data on the intermediate target must be readily available on a timely basis. An aggregate not measured until long afterward is of little operational value. Moreover, the relevant data must be not only available but also reasonably reliable.

I have recently proposed a *credit* target for U.S. monetary policy because my research has indicated that at least one specific credit aggregate, *total net credit* (the outstanding indebtedness of all U.S. nonfinancial borrowers), satisfactorily meets each of these four criteria. Before proceeding to such a conclusion, it is essential to ask at the outset, "satisfactory" in comparison to what? Because the current framework used by the Federal Reserve System relies on monetary aggregate targets, the immediate standard required to support a proposal for change is that the proposed new target must meet these four criteria at least as well as do the monetary aggregates that are the current focus of monetary policy. The relationship between total net credit and both real income and price measures of nonfinancial economic activity, judged by a variety of different statistical approaches, is as stable and reliable as is the corresponding relationship for any of the monetary aggregates (or the monetary base). The information about subsequent movements in nonfinancial activity contained in total net credit is at least comparable to that contained in money. Relationships between total net credit and either the quantity of nonborrowed reserves or the federal funds rate are comparable to the corresponding relationships for the principal monetary aggregates. Finally, data for a close approximation to total net credit are available on a monthly basis, and the relevant relationships based on the monthly data are also at least comparable to the corresponding relationships for the monetary aggregates.

The Federal Reserve System should therefore adopt an explicit *two-target* framework in which it would focus both on the money stock and on the quantity of credit outstanding. The Federal Reserve System should pick one monetary aggregate, presumably M1, and one credit aggregate, total net credit; specify target ranges for both; and provide the quantity of reserves (or set a short-term interest rate) aimed at achieving these two targets. A deviation of either money or credit growth from its respective target range would then constitute a signal warranting reassessment of that reserve provision path (or interest rate level).

One potential difficulty in implementing this hybrid money-and-credit framework is a problem inherently associated with any policy of pursuing two targets instead of one. What if both targets are not simultaneously achievable? For all practical purposes, however, the Federal Reserve System's current policy framework already suffers from just this problem, as the experience of M1 and M2 during 1981 demonstrated. If only M1 had mattered, the Federal Reserve System would have had to conclude early on that its policy was too restrictive in relation to the specified target. By contrast, if only M2 had mattered, it would have had to draw the opposite conclusion. In resolving these conflicting concerns, the Federal Reserve System had to decide on the relative importance of M1 and M2 and to determine why one was growing more slowly than anticipated and the other more rapidly.

A two-target framework based jointly on money and credit would in part have the same features. If money and credit were both growing in line with their respective targets, then the Federal Reserve System would judge the prevailing reserve provision path (or short-term interest rate) to be appropriate. If both were above target, then the implication would be to slow the provision of reserves (or raise the interest rate). If both were below target, the implication would be to speed the reserve provision path (or lower the interest rate). If one were above target and one below, however, then—just as now, with an M1 and M2 target—the Federal Reserve System would have to assess which was more important under the circumstances and determine why one was moving in one direction and one in the opposite direction relative to their respective stated targets.

The key advantage of an explicit two-target framework on both money and credit, in comparison to a two-target approach based on two separate definitions of the money stock, is that it would draw on a more diverse information base to generate the set of signals that presumptively matter for monetary policy. Money is, after all, an asset held by the public, and each monetary aggregate is just a separate subtotal of the public's monetary assets. By having an M1 and an M2 target, as at present, the Federal Reserve System is relying solely on the *asset* side of the economy's balance sheet but adding up those assets in two separate ways. By having a money target and a credit target, the Federal Reserve System would create a presumption of responding to signals from *both* sides of the economy's balance sheet. The evidence that is now available indicates—not surprisingly, on some reflection—that both sides of the balance sheet do matter.

Finally, as a practical matter it is useful to note that the Federal Reserve System is free to implement this two-target money-and-credit policy framework at any time. No legislation is necessary. On the contrary, the Humphrey-Hawkins Act of 1978 directs the Federal Reserve System to specify a target for credit growth as well as for money growth. The Federal Open Market Committee has typically specified such a target, but it has chosen to focus only on credit extended through the banking system, which the available evidence indicates is far from the best source of information about the economy, even from within the liability side of the balance sheet. Moreover, the Federal Reserve System's own discussions of monetary policy—in its reports to Congress, in the Federal Open Market Committee's policy directives, and elsewhere —make clear that the focus of policy is on money, not credit. Nothing in the legislation, however, requires that the Federal Reserve System place its primary emphasis on money to the exclusion of credit or that it focus only on bank credit among the available credit measures. From a legislative perspective, a

two-target money-and-credit framework would simply have the
Federal Reserve System be even-handed within the requirements
already laid down by the Humphrey-Hawkins Act of 1978.

CHOOSING AN OPERATING PROCEDURE

One of the greatest misperceptions surrounding the implementation of monetary policy today concerns the Federal Reserve
System's ability to affect its monetary aggregate targets. The
popular press, and even many supposedly informed observers,
continually write or speak as if the central bank created (or with-
drew) money in the economy at will, so that movements of any
given monetary aggregate always reflected policy actions by the
Federal Reserve System. In the extreme, monthly and sometimes
even weekly movements in the Ms are taken to be results directly
sought by monetary policy, and the Federal Reserve System's
motives are questioned accordingly.

In fact, in a fractional reserve banking system like that of the
United States, "money" is *not* the direct liability of the Federal
Reserve System, nor do its actions directly control the money stock.
Even M1, the narrowest of the monetary aggregates, represents the
liabilities of some 40,000 banks and other depository institutions,
and the broader monetary aggregates also include such items as
shares in money market mutual funds. The amount of money in
the economy at any given time is the net result of portfolio decisions taken by all of these institutions issuing monetary liabilities,
as well as by millions of individuals and businesses holding monetary assets.

The Federal Reserve System can, of course, importantly affect
the amount of money that banks and other institutions create and
that individuals and businesses hold. It does so primarily by means
of open market operations. These purchases and sales of securities
govern the amount of reserves available to back reservable deposits
(which constitute most of any M measure) and thereby influence
the level of market interest rates. Because the lending decisions
of banks and other money-issuing institutions depend on interest
rates, as do the portfolio preferences of money-holding individuals
and businesses, the Federal Reserve System's control over open

market operations gives it an important lever with which to affect the growth of any monetary (or credit) aggregate.

That control is not very precise, however, and the shorter the time frame the less precise it typically is. Achieving the degree of control implied by the Federal Reserve System's reporting its money growth targets to Congress on an annual basis and with a leeway of three percentage points (for example, 2.5 to 5.5 percent growth in M1 for 1982) is apparently quite plausible in light of the available evidence. By contrast, close control over a single month, or even a calendar quarter, is probably not achievable.

What, then, can the Federal Reserve System control precisely? Apart from the discount rate and the required reserve ratios, both of which are technical devices of limited importance (for purposes of monetary policy) in the modern banking system, the only two options the Federal Reserve System has in this context are to set the quantity or the price at which it executes open market operations—that is, to set reserves or a short-term interest rate. One possible operating procedure begins by deciding how rapidly to expand or contract the system's reserves. Because adding reserves is identical to making open market purchases and withdrawing reserves is identical to making open market sales, under this procedure the Federal Reserve System would execute a fixed quantity of open market purchases or sales and leave to the market the resulting interest rate. The other possible operating procedure begins by simply deciding what short-term interest rate level should prevail. Because the interest rate on a security is just the inverse of its price, under that procedure the Federal Reserve System would execute whatever quantity of purchases or sales (and, hence, add or withdraw whatever quantity of reserves) the market sought at the fixed rate.

At least over short time horizons, the Federal Reserve System can conduct open market operations by either of these alternatives. (In the long run, however, the interest rate setting alternative would probably not be feasible.) The essence of the choice between the two is to determine which procedure gives better control over the monetary or credit aggregate used as the intermediate target of monetary policy and also which procedure has the least undesirable side effects on the general functioning of the financial markets.

When the Federal Reserve System first adopted money growth targets in the 1970s, it used an operating procedure based on setting the federal funds rate (the interest rate on overnight bank reserves) at the level judged appropriate for achieving the targeted growth for the monetary aggregates. In October 1979, however, the Federal Reserve System changed to the alternative procedure based on setting the growth of reserves (that is, again, the quantity of open market transactions) and leaving short-term interest rates to fluctuate freely in the market. The stated reason for this change was the expectation that the new procedure would result in closer control over the monetary aggregates.

In fact, however, control over the monetary aggregates has not improved at all but has actually deteriorated since October 1979. The increased volatility of the Ms during this period may have been due, of course, to factors other than the change in operating procedure. Some additional volatility may have resulted from specific financial innovations, for example. Nevertheless, the positive contribution of the new procedure remains unproved. Moreover—and remarkably enough in light of widespread public presumptions—the limited evidence available before the October 1979 change never offered much support for the new procedure in the first place. The evidence was sufficiently mixed to make the new experiment worth trying, but not to warrant much surprise if it failed.

Meanwhile, as almost any analysis of monetary policy would have predicted, the short-run volatility of short-term interest rates increased immediately and dramatically after the adoption of the new procedure. In addition, the volatility of long-term interest rates also increased. Not only has the amplitude of interest rate swings during the economy's subsequent business cycles been unprecedented in U.S. financial experience, but the volatility of interest rates over shorter time horizons—month-to-month, day-to-day, and even within the trading day—has also increased sharply.

Because significantly greater interest rate volatility increases financial risks and therefore increases risk premiums and, therefore, borrowing costs along the lines indicated in the discussion above, the chief question that arises in this context is whether the advantages gained by the October 1979 change in operating procedure have been worth the costs. The costs involved are simply the increase in risk and consequent erosion of smoothly functioning markets that have followed the increase in interest rate volatility. By contrast, the advantages, in principle involving superior Federal Reserve System control over the monetary aggregates, have not been apparent. Moreover, the available evidence also does *not* support the claim that further institutional changes like that from a lagged to a contemporaneous reserve accounting basis, scheduled to take effect in 1983, will make much difference either.

In sum, the time has also come to rethink the October 1979 change to a reserve-based operating procedure for monetary policy. The resulting increase in short-run interest rate volatility has been pronounced, but it has not obviously brought an improvement in monetary control—nor, for that matter, any other apparent gain. In the absence of some clear benefit from this procedure, which does impose significant costs on the financial markets and the economy more generally, the Federal Reserve System should at least consider tempering the procedure so as to eliminate some part of the additional short-run interest rate volatility.

Summary of Conclusions

Monetary policy in the United States has been in a period of transition since the 1970s, and there are reasons to believe that this transition is not—indeed, should not be—complete. The main changes in the Federal Reserve System's conduct of monetary policy during this period, first to a strategy focused on monetary targets and then to an operating procedure based on bank reserves, were consistent with the requirements of the new inflationary financial environment. Other new factors in the economy, however, including the more rapid pace of financial innovation and the increased importance of supply-side shocks, operate against this formula for conducting monetary policy. At least some further changes in the monetary policy framework are necessary.

Pursuit of unrealistic goals can lead to poor policy. Monetary policy can reduce price inflation, but not without costs measured by foregone output and incomes and by a poorer environment for business capital formation. Except for temporary periods like the course of a disinflation, however, monetary policy probably cannot directly affect the economy's net investment performance to any significant extent. By contrast, monetary policy can support capital formation indirectly, even on an ongoing basis, by maintaining financial conditions conducive to smoothly functioning markets and reduced levels of risk.

Monetary policy is just one part of the overall economy's system of macroeconomic management along with, in the first instance, fiscal policy. The simultaneous pursuit of intertwined goals by interrelated policy instruments clearly raises the need for some coordination between them. The principles of a democratic republic indicate that Congress and the President have the authority to determine the nation's broad macroeconomic objectives, and the Federal Reserve System is responsible for conducting monetary policy within those objectives. Although informal consultations will probably have to continue to carry much of the burden of fiscal-monetary coordination, one useful formal step would be for Congress to require the Federal Reserve System, as part of the chairman's semiannual reports under the Humphrey-Hawkins Act of 1978, to state precisely the set of basic macroeconomic objectives underlying its current monetary policy stance.

On narrowly economic grounds, a monetary policy approach relating Federal Reserve System actions directly to desired macroeconomic outcomes would be superior to a system based on intermediate targets. For political reasons, however, both Congress and the Federal Reserve System appear firmly committed to at least some kind of intermediate target system which can provide accountability of monetary policy through an ongoing monitoring process. Even so, conditions now prevailing and likely to prevail throughout the 1980s do not favor the current approach based exclusively on the monetary aggregates.

The Federal Reserve System should adopt an explicit two-target framework in which it would focus both on the money stock and on the quantity of credit outstanding. It should pick one monetary aggregate, presumably M1, and one credit aggregate, total net credit; specify target ranges for both; and provide the quantity of reserves (or set a short-term interest rate) aimed at achieving these two targets. A deviation of either money or credit growth from its respective target range would then constitute a signal warranting reassessment of that reserve provision path (or interest rate level).

The key advantage of an explicit two-target framework based on both money and credit, in comparison to the current policy based on monetary aggregates only, is that it would draw on a more diverse information base to generate the set of signals governing the systematic response of monetary policy to economic events.

Finally, the October 1979 change to a reserve-based operating procedure for monetary policy has increased short-run interest rate volatility, which imposes costs on financial institutions as well as on others who use the economy's financial markets, but has not brought any apparent gain in monetary control. The Federal Reserve System should therefore seek ways to modify its operating procedure so as to eliminate some part of the additional short-run interest rate volatility.

Isabel V. Sawhill

5

Human Resources

The performance of the American economy was disappointing during the 1970s. Prices more than doubled over the decade and productivity growth slowed and finally came to a virtual halt. Over 18 million additional jobs were created but employment did not grow as fast as the labor force with the result that unemployment was higher at each cyclical peak. Reversing these trends will require a sustained effort on many fronts, involving more investment, better coordination of fiscal and monetary policies, and more attention to the costs and benefits of alternative means of achieving public purposes. Success will also hinge on rethinking public and private strategies for developing, motivating, and utilizing human resources.

This chapter addresses four issues in the human resources area. First, based on current demographic projections, how many jobs

ISABEL V. SAWHILL *is a senior fellow at* The Urban Institute. *Formerly she was program director for employment and labor policy there and was also the director of the National Commission for Employment Policy. Dr. Sawhill 'has written numerous articles and books and coedited* Youth Employment and Public Policy *and* The Reagan Experiment: An Examination of Economic and Social Policies under the Reagan Administration. *The author wishes to thank Diana Roth for her assistance with this chapter. The author also wants to acknowledge the comments received from a number of people, especially Francis D. Fisher, Eli Ginzberg, Sar Levitan, Steven M. Miller, Michael O'Keefe, James O'Toole, William Ouchi, Jerome M. Rosow, Frank W. Schiff, and Laurence Steinberg. The findings and conclusions are the author's alone.*

are likely to be needed, and for whom, over the next several decades? Second, where will the jobs be and how are shifts in demand and new technologies likely to affect the industrial and occupational structure of the labor force? Third, what kinds of education and training will be needed to prepare the labor force for these changes and improve the rate of productivity growth? Finally, can new institutional mechanisms be developed that give workers more of a stake in the economic success of their enterprises and the economy as a whole, thereby reducing inflationary wage pressures and resistance to technological change? The answers to this last question are both the most difficult and the most important. In the absence of a means of controlling inflation that relies less on maintaining high levels of unemployment, economic growth is likely to be weak or sporadic. Similarly, the technological preeminence that will be needed to sustain advances in productivity and standards of living in an increasingly competitive world economy could be frustrated by popular concerns about job security and technological unemployment.

The New Demographics

In any society there are some groups deemed too old, too young, or too incapacitated to work. Others have been socially exempted from regular employment by their involvement in schooling, homemaking, or military service. Unless they have considerable savings, these groups must be supported by the working population. Such support may be provided directly (through the earnings of another family member) or indirectly (through taxes and transfers). Two trends have been in evidence in most industrialized countries: (1) a shift in the composition of the "dependent population" from adult women to younger and older males and (2) a shift in the support of this population from private (family) to public sources.

In the United States at the beginning of this century, about 31 percent of the entire population was in the labor force. By mid-century this ratio had risen to 42 percent, and by 1980, 47 percent, with a still higher ratio predicted for the year 2000. Offsetting this tendency for a higher fraction of the population to be employed

102   *Isabel V. Sawhill*

has been a decline in nonmarket economic activity (e.g., home production of food or clothes) and in lifetime hours worked per person.

The composition of the nonworking population has shifted, especially since World War II. A far larger proportion are over sixty-five, and fewer are adult women. These changes in composition are the direct result of the increased tendency for women to work outside the home and for men to retire at earlier ages (Table 1).

TABLE 1. CIVILIAN LABOR FORCE PARTICIPATION RATES

	Male				Female			
	Total 16+	*16–24*	*25–54*	*55+*	*Total 16+*	*16–24*	*25–54*	*55+*
1950	87	77	96	68	34	43	36	19
1980	78	74	94	45	52	61	63	23
2000	75	75	92	37	56	72	72	19

Sources: Compiled from: 1950, U.S. Census; 1980, Bureau of Labor Statistics; 2000, Bureau of Labor Statistics midlevel projections from U.S. Census data, unpublished.

Over half of all adult women and 62 percent of those under age fifty-five are now in the labor force. These proportions are likely to continue to increase as successive generations of younger women with more "liberated" attitudes enter and move into their adult years. The shift in attitudes has been dramatic and is not likely to be reversed. In 1968, 62 percent of young women between the ages of fourteen and twenty-two reported that they planned to be housewives. By 1979, the proportion had fallen to 20 percent. Other factors that may contribute to more employment among women include rising education, smaller families, more divorce, and the need to have two paychecks to purchase the ever-elusive "American dream." Elsewhere Kristin Moore and I have discussed the implications of the increased employment of women for home and family life. Suffice it to say here that the growing number of two-career families is likely to generate new consumption patterns and demands for more flexible working hours and for greater public subsidization (through tax credits or otherwise) of day care or preprimary education. The consequences of greater female employment for the economy include a higher measured gross national product (GNP) and the tax revenues to finance, among other things, extended retirement benefits for the elderly and educational benefits for the young. Productivity, as conventionally measured, may have been adversely affected by the entry of older, inexperienced women into the labor force in recent years, but younger women are increasingly making the same kind of permanent commitment to the labor force as young men. In any case, any adverse effect will be more than offset in the next decade by the aging of the labor force as the baby boom matures. Moreover, real economic welfare should rise to the extent that women have been underemployed at home.

Almost as revolutionary as the increased employment of women has been the trend toward earlier retirement among men. In 1950, 63 percent of men, aged fifty-five or over, were in the labor force. By 1980 the proportion had fallen to 45 percent, and by the year 2000, it is projected to be 37 percent. Older men are working less because of greater affluence and more generous Social Security benefits, pensions, and disability insurance.

The amount of economic dependency in the future will depend critically on the extent to which older Americans choose to work. The fiscal squeeze which a graying America is putting on the Social Security System will likely lead to shifts in policy that encourage more work effort among the elderly. The age at which people become eligible for Social Security, the level of benefits, and the extent to which benefits are reduced for those who continue to work past the age of eligibility all affect retirement decisions. Changes in these policies, together with other factors (such as greater longevity, improved health, or continuing inflation) could easily reverse the present trend toward earlier retirement.

Based on one reasonable set of assumptions about future labor force participation rates, Figure 1 compares the composition of the work force in the year 2000 to the current situation. Overall, the labor force will be 27 percent (or about 29 million people) larger than it is today. It will also be older, with the average age increasing from thirty-five to thirty-eight years. Finally, it will have a higher proportion of women and ethnic minorities.

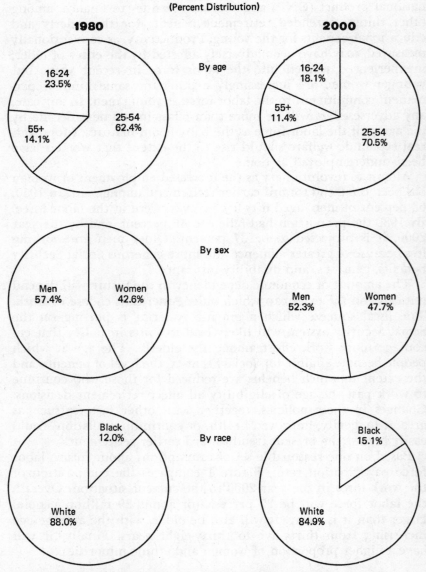

Fig. 1. *Composition of the Labor Force, 1980 and 2000*

(Percent Distribution)

1980

2000

By age

16-24
23.5%

25-54
62.4%

55+
14.1%

16-24
18.1%

55+
11.4%

25-54
70.5%

By sex

Men
57.4%

Women
42.6%

Men
52.3%

Women
47.7%

By race

Black
12.0%

White
88.0%

Black
15.1%

White
84.9%

Sources: U.S. Bureau of Census and U.S. Bureau of Labor Statistics.

Job Opportunities and the Challenge of Technology

Over the next two decades, the economy will need to generate enough additional jobs to absorb both a growing labor force and the workers whose jobs are displaced by technology and other advances in productivity. If labor productivity (output per person) were to advance by a healthy 2 percent a year, we would need to produce 64 million new jobs between 1980 and 2000—about half of these to provide opportunities for workers potentially "displaced" by the assumed growth in productivity and about half to accommodate the projected growth in the labor force. To achieve this goal, GNP would need to grow at a rate of 3.2 percent a year, on average, considerably higher than the 2.4 percent growth rate achieved between 1973 and 1980 but a little lower than the 3.5 percent rate achieved for the entire post–World War II period. Greater productivity advances or a higher labor force participation rate would require stronger GNP growth than this or else a willingness to tolerate more unemployment than in the past. The latter is always a possibility, given continuing fears of inflation and the growing public perception that unemployment creates little hardship, because of the greater availability of jobless benefits and other sources of income support for the unemployed. But tolerating higher unemployment entails producing fewer goods and services and accepting lower standards of living.

There is, of course, a rate of unemployment that represents some frictional or structural minimum not amenable to a macro-economic solution. Two unemployment rates need to be distinguished in this connection. The first is the unemployment rate at which inflation begins to accelerate. The second is the unemployment rate at which there is an overall balance between demand and supply in the labor market. In recent years, such factors as rising oil prices, increasing payroll taxes, and the productivity slowdown have caused inflation to accelerate long before there was excess demand in the labor market and have led some economists to conclude that the "full employment unemployment rate"—defined as the rate needed to prevent accelerating inflation —has risen to 7 or 8 percent. But this is simply the amount of unemployment that would be needed to offset the inflationary impact of such "supply shocks" and in no sense represents full employment. In absence of such supply shocks, and given an expected decline in youth employment as the baby boom generation matures, the macro managers should be able to safely aim at an unemployment rate of between 5 and 6 percent in the future. Since unemployment has been higher than this since the end of 1979, the economy will need to grow at a faster than average pace during the 1980s before it reaches and then advances along its full-employment growth path. Even the most optimistic economic projections suggest that it will not reach this full-employment level before the second half of the 1980s.

Assuming that an adequate number of total jobs is generated, where will these jobs be? The answer depends on (1) future expenditure patterns which will cause some sectors of the economy to expand more rapidly than others and (2) shifts in technology or other factors which affect the amount of labor needed to satisfy that demand.

Some of the shifts in consumer, business, and government purchases that can be expected in the future include more spending for defense goods (because of changing national priorities), more for health care and less for education (because of the aging of the population), and more for consumer durables and recreation (because of rising incomes). Based on these projections of demand, the Bureau of Labor Statistics (BLS) estimates total output and employment by detailed industry (making certain assumptions about industry productivity growth and the extent to which each industry utilizes inputs from other industries). These industry projections are then translated into a set of occupational projections based on current occupational staffing patterns within industries. The resulting estimates are clearly subject to considerable error. Nevertheless, they provide some indication of where the jobs of the future will be (Table 2):

1. About 50 percent of all workers now hold white-collar jobs, up from 36 percent in 1950. These jobs will continue to grow more rapidly than other jobs over the next decade. However, clerical and managerial jobs will grow somewhat more slowly than sales and professional jobs.

2. About 33 percent of the work force is currently in blue-collar occupations, down from 41 percent in 1950. Labor-saving technological change will mean a slower-than-average growth rate of jobs in unskilled and semiskilled operative and laborer occupations. The demand for skilled craft workers should remain strong.

3. Only about 15 percent of all workers are currently employed in the service sector, but this has been, and will continue to be, the fastest growing source of new jobs.
4. Three percent of all workers are now employed in farming, and further declines are anticipated.

TABLE 2. THE JOB OUTLOOK

| | *(Employment in thousands)* | | | | | | *Percent Change* | |
| | *1950* | | *1980* | | *1990* | | | |
	Number of Workers	*Percent of All Workers*	*Number of Workers*	*Percent of All Workers*	*Number of Workers*	*Percent of All Workers*	*1950 to 1980*	*1980 to 1990*
White collar	21,601	36	51,436	50	62,753	50	138	22
Blue collar	24,266	41	32,435	32	39,018	32	33	20
Service	6,180	10	15,547	15	19,668	16	151	26
Farm	6,953	13	2,689	3	2,309	2	–61	–14

Sources: Compiled from Bureau of Labor Statistics, *Occupational Outlook Quarterly,* Spring 1982 and Bureau of the Census, *Historical Statistics, Colonial Times to 1970,* Series D 182–232.

Some observers are predicting that a new industrial revolution, centered around computer-based technologies and microelectronically controlled equipment (e.g., robots, word processors), will take place during the next thirty years and lead to widespread displacement of less skilled workers by machines. Assembly line workers and low-level clerical employees would likely be the most affected.

Estimates of the number of industrial robots in the United States suggest that they are being introduced at a rapid pace but are still performing a small proportion of all manufacturing jobs. (The word robot was adopted from the Czech word *robota,* meaning serf. A robot differs from other automated equipment in that it is computer-controlled and can be reprogramed to perform a variety of tasks.) There are now about 5,000 to 6,000 robots in the U.S., up from an estimated 200 in 1970 and 2,000 in 1975. Some financial analysts and industry spokespersons predict there may well be over 100,000 by 1990. Assuming one robot replaced three workers (because the robot can work all three shifts), this would still be less than 3 percent of all production jobs in manufacturing. Based on a survey of firms, Robert V. Ayres and Steven M. Miller in their study *Robotics: Applications and Social Implications,* suggest that it might be technologically feasible to use the next generation of robots (those with rudimentary vision and other sensory capabilities) to replace as many as 4 million factory workers or 3 to 4 percent of all jobs in the economy within the next twenty years. But this is a very uncertain estimate which does not take into account whether this degree of automation would be economically profitable.

In certain industries, firms, and types of work there will be a much greater concentration of robots than the above averages would imply. About half of all robots are currently employed in the auto industry—largely in painting and welding operations—and almost all of the rest are employed in three other durable goods industries (fabricated metals, machinery, and electrical equipment). These industries are heavily concentrated in the Great Lakes states, New York, and California. Some individual firms have been particularly aggressive in their use of robots. For example, General Motors hopes to install at least 14,000 robots by 1990. The economic incentives are compelling. In 1981, it cost about six dollars an hour to employ a robot in the automotive industry. This compares to a labor cost of seventeen dollars an hour in the same industry. These savings mean that investment in a robot typically pays for itself in a year or two. If, as expected, the price of robots falls and the cost of labor rises, automation will become even more attractive.

On the office front, sales of word processors have been rising by 50 percent a year since 1975, but the more fully automated office of the future with an interconnected system of desk-top terminals or "work stations" has been slow to arrive. While most users believe that word processors and other automated office equipment improve employee productivity, there is no firm evidence as yet to support this claim.

While the foregoing discussion suggests that new technologies are being introduced at a rapid pace, fears of massive dislocations and widespread unemployment hardly seem warranted. Much of the problem of displacement could be taken care of by normal attrition. In manufacturing, between 25 and 35 percent of the labor force quits voluntarily, retires, or is discharged each year.

Moreover, both history and economic logic suggest that rapid productivity growth produces more rather than fewer employment opportunities. In 1770 Britain's textile industry was mechanized, and by 1800 employment in that industry had increased by 350 percent. Similarly, after Henry Ford introduced assembly line production of the automobile in 1910, employment grew by 450 percent over the next ten years. Between 1955 and 1976 employment rose three times as fast in five high-technology industries as it did in all other industries, according to the Machinery and Allied Products Association. Other studies of the effects of automation on employment in such industries as aluminum, autos, foundries, metalworking machinery, and electric and electronic equipment have come to similar, though somewhat less optimistic, conclusions.

The reason for these favorable outcomes is that lower costs and prices due to technological advances often stimulate demand and expand market shares for those in the forefront of change. For example, Japan currently has about three times as many robots as the United States, and this may be one reason for its inroads into U.S. markets in recent years. Just as no individual firm can afford to ignore the latest cost-saving techniques, no country can fail to maintain its competitive edge in world markets.

Automation not only promises to increase employment opportunities but could also support higher wages as industry becomes more capital intensive. In addition, the use of robots will eliminate the boring, unpleasant, and dangerous jobs that are unpopular with workers.

Although the benefits of technology are substantial, there will be costs imposed on those individuals whose jobs are eliminated and a need for public or private response to the problems. But, as discussed below, this is only one of the challenges that the education and training system must meet over the coming decades.

Education and Training

The United States spends somewhere in the neighborhood of $220 billion annually for education and training (Table 3), or 8 percent of GNP (1980 dollars). This compares with $296 billion for plant and equipment investment (11 percent of GNP).

TABLE 3. TOTAL EXPENDITURES ON EDUCATION AND TRAINING IN THE UNITED
          STATES

	Estimated Expenditures (Billions of Dollars)*	Percent
Total	220	100
Elementary and secondary education	107	49
Postsecondary education	59	27
Private business and industry	30	13
Federal employment and training programs (all agencies)	14	6
Federal government, civilian, and military training	10	5

* Most figures are for 1980 but the estimates come from different sources and some—particularly those for business and industry expenditures—are only rough guesses.

Sources: Compiled from National Commission for Employment Policy, *Seventh Annual Report,* Chapter 4 and U.S. National Center for Education Statistics, *Digest of Education Statistics.*

About half of the expenditures are for elementary and secondary education (90 percent of which is publicly financed, mostly with state and local dollars). The next largest chunk is for higher education, followed by business and industry expenditures on training (the latter being by far the most difficult to estimate). Finally, as a relatively small component of the total, are the federal government's outlays on such programs as CETA (the Comprehensive Employment and Training Act), WIN (an employment program for welfare recipients), and the Employment Service (a public employment agency). The federal government also provides substantial training to its own civilian and military employees. In 1980, for example, the military spent $8 billion on training, or as much as the entire CETA program.

What have these investments produced? We first examine education and then the federally-supported training programs.

EDUCATION

The overall education level of the population has risen substantially since World War II. The illiteracy rate declined from 3 percent in 1947 to 0.5 percent in 1979. Median school years completed by those twenty-five and over rose from 9.3 years in 1950 to 12.5 years in 1980.

In addition to its obvious and important noneconomic benefits, education contributes to economic growth in a number of ways. It enables individual workers to perform on the job. It produces new scientific knowledge and aids in the rapid diffusion or application of that knowledge to the production process. And it facilitates adjustment to change since educated workers are more adaptable and more easily retrained and educated managers are more receptive to new ideas.

Historically, increased education has been an important source of productivity growth. As shown in Table 4, it accounted for

TABLE 4. CONTRIBUTIONS OF EDUCATION TO THE GROWTH OF PRODUCTIVITY IN THE UNITED STATES

	Average Annual Percentage Changes for Nonresidential Business Sector	
	1948–1973	*1973–1981*
National income per person employed	2.5	−0.2
Education	0.5	0.6
Capital	0.4	0.2
All other	1.6	−1.0

Source: Based on information from Edward F. Denison, "The Interruption of Productivity Growth in the United States," paper prepared for Conference of the Royal Economic Society, London, July 22, 1982, Table 2.

20 percent of the growth of national income per person employed between 1948 and 1973. Since 1973, this particular measure of productivity has actually fallen. However, in the absence of a continued rise in the educational qualifications of those entering the private business sector over this period, the decline in productivity would have been even greater. During both periods, investment in education contributed more than investment in plant and equipment and other forms of tangible capital to productivity growth.

The impact of education on growth is measured by examining changes in years of schooling completed by the labor force weighted by the earnings associated with different levels of education. Thus, as long as educational attainment is rising because each age cohort entering the labor force is somewhat better educated than previous generations, the contribution of education will be positive. It is possible, however, that this increase in the quality of education has been at least partially offset by a decline in quality. People may be going to school longer but learning less each year.

This hypothesis is supported by evidence from various standardized tests as well as by complaints from employers and college teachers about recent school graduates. Until 1981, Scholastic Aptitude Test (SAT) scores had been declining since the mid–1960s. The average verbal score dropped 13 percent (from 479 in 1963 to 424 in 1980), and the average math score dropped 8 percent (from 502 to 466). Some, but not all, of the decline is due to the broader cross section of the population taking the test.

Similarly disquieting evidence comes from periodic surveys of the educational achievements of a national sample of students at ages nine, thirteen, and seventeen (the National Assessment of Educational Progress). Some gains have been scored by the youngest age group, but among seventeen-year olds, there have been declines in mathematical skills, in reading comprehension, and in knowledge of science and social science since the tests were first administered in the early 1970s. Some illustrative findings from recent surveys are:

1. About 25 percent of seventeen-year olds do not know the number of quarts in a gallon, the number of ounces in a pound, and the number of feet in a yard.
2. Forty percent do not know what percent thirty is of sixty, that more than 100 percent of a number is greater than the number itself, or how to calculate the area of a square when the length of only one side is given.
3. More than 50 percent could not name their congressperson or one of their senators, and 20 percent did not know that senators are elected.
4. Only 44 percent of seventeen-year olds could successfully combine four short sentences into one longer one.

How do American students compare with those in other countries? In a sixteen-nation survey of educational attainment, conducted by the International Association for the Evaluation of Educational Achievement, American secondary school students ranked third from the bottom in reading and in science and ranked the lowest in math among industrialized countries. It should be noted that at age fourteen, American students perform comparatively well. Their poor showing at the secondary level reflects, in part, the larger proportion of less able students who complete secondary school in the United States.

These declines in American performance have been attributed to a variety of factors in addition to the broadening of educational opportunities to include less able students. Often cited are television and less parental supervision, an insufficiently demanding curriculum at the secondary level, declining college entrance requirements and admission standards, competing demands on students' time (including employment), and the qualifications of teachers. Some of the relevant facts are:

1. A majority of seventeen-year-olds spend less than five hours a week on homework and watch at least seven hours a week of television.
2. Over 50 percent of all high school juniors and seniors are employed at any one time during the school year. While working has some benefits, recent evidence suggests that spending more than fifteen to twenty hours at work tends to impair school performance.
3. About two-thirds of U.S. colleges and universities are now providing remedial reading and writing courses.
4. Publishers have been forced to water down and simplify the material in college textbooks.
5. College seniors majoring in education have lower SAT scores than students in all other fields with the exception of office-clerical and vocational-technical fields. The scores of education majors declined over the past decade as high-ability females and minorities opted for other careers. Teacher verbal ability has been clearly linked to student test performance.
6. Teacher salaries more than kept pace with other salaries between 1960 and 1978. Currently, the average secondary school teacher earns $18,000. This compares to $17,000 for carpenters and $21,000 for postal clerks. More importantly, there is little earnings progression with increased experience and little differentiation of rewards among those with different abilities, responsibilities, or competing opportunities. Math and science teachers, for example, are deserting the schools for more lucrative jobs in industry. Able teachers in all fields reportedly leave because of their dissatisfaction with the bureaucratic organizations of the schools, classroom violence, and other working conditions.

The solutions to the problems in our educational system are not self-evident. More than an infusion of new money is needed. Education expenditures per student enrolled in elementary and secondary school doubled in real terms between 1960 and 1975 and then leveled off at the same time that test scores were declining. Educational experts seem to be unsure about what policies to recommend, but some reform of the curriculum (already underway in some high schools) and of the basic organization of schools and structure of the teaching profession may be needed. Setting higher standards and testing competencies against these standards could also help.

One potentially interesting, though largely untested, idea is the introduction of more computers into the classroom. Computer-assisted instruction has a number of putative benefits. Because it is interactive, it motivates students and actively engages them in the learning process. It corrects their mistakes in a nonthreatening manner. It can be paced to accommodate individual differences in ability but use software incorporating the most sophisticated knowledge, and up-to-date pedagogical techniques, with built-in performance standards. It can free teachers to help students develop critical problem-solving skills and humanistic values. And it can help to develop computer literacy—the essential "fourth R" in a technologically advanced nation. At present, the bottlenecks appear to be (1) cost, (2) inertia, (3) the insecurity of teachers unfamiliar with the new technology, and most importantly (4) a lack of high-quality software. Unless schools move rapidly, there may soon be more computers in the home than in the classroom, increasing the already extensive educational advantages of the middle class and creating a nation of video game addicts rather than a new generation of Nobel Prize winning scientists.

It appears that the era of rapidly expanding educational attainment is over. Past progress was sustained by an increase in the proportion of each successive birth cohort that entered and then graduated from high school. Because such a high proportion of young people now graduates from high school, further significant increases in educational attainment will only come with higher rates of college attendance. An issue for the coming decades, then, is whether universal college education is desirable and who should pay for it.

The current and projected surplus of college-trained youth will undoubtedly affect how this issue is resolved. During the 1970s, 20 percent of college graduates took jobs that traditionally have not required a college degree. As a result, the proportion holding professional and technical occupations fell from 67 percent in 1970 to 55 percent in 1980 as employers raised their hiring standards in nonprofessional occupations and job seekers were forced to lower their expectations. The BLS projects a similar condition of oversupply and occupation downgrading during the 1980s, even under relatively optimistic assumptions about economic growth. In short, although many young people will continue to seek a college education for its many noneconomic benefits and the competitive edge it provides in vying for entry-level jobs, it is questionable whether society should encourage still greater participation in higher education. An alternative strategy would be (1) to improve the quality of existing education, especially at the secondary level, and (2) to provide more mid-career education and training opportunities for adults with specific occupational and career objectives. The large influx of mature students into higher education institutions in recent years (38 percent are now over twenty-five) attests to the growing needs and interests of this group.

TRAINING

As we have seen (Table 3), most training in the U.S. is provided by private employers. Federally supported training programs have been on a relatively small scale and heavily focused on the disadvantaged. As Eli Ginzberg has put it, they represent "second-chance" opportunities for low-income minority youth, welfare recipients, and others with special needs. Critics have labeled these programs "make-work" or "income maintenance in disguise."

Some are now urging that the federal government expand its role to provide more training opportunities for all workers, not just the disadvantaged. What are the arguments for and against federal involvement in serving various groups, and what is the evidence that this involvement has been a good use of taxpayer dollars?

Assisting the Disadvantaged—Assisting the disadvantaged has been an important objective of federal employment and training efforts ever since the mid–1960s and became the primary objective after the reauthorization of CETA in 1978. New legislation enacted in 1982 would not change this basic orientation but would emphasize different forms of assistance and more private sector involvement. In particular, there is now less interest in providing income transfers through temporary work experience programs and more on improving long-term earnings and employability via training. This shift is consistent with evidence indicating that CETA work experience and public service employment have been less cost-effective than classroom and on-the-job training programs. Similarly, relatively resource-intensive remedial training programs have proven more beneficial than summer job programs in improving the long-term earnings of disadvantaged youth. In short, although training programs tend to be more expensive per person served, they also tend to yield a higher rate of return for the participants and the taxpayer.

One program which has been quite effective is the Job Corps, a program designed to provide training for disadvantaged, hard-to-employ youth. After a long process of development, the program appears to have found a successful means of improving basic literacy as well as job skills. The social rate of return for program participants is estimated to be about 45 percent. Sixty percent of the total benefits takes the form of increased output and earnings while most of the rest is attributed to reduced criminal activity. As further evidence of its success, the program's training techniques are being adopted by the military and other institutions dealing with disadvantaged youth.

A second program which has been partially successful in dealing with the disadvantaged is the Supported Work Demonstration Project. This project focused on four hard-to-employ groups: welfare mothers (women receiving Aid to Families with Dependent

Children—AFDC), problem youths, exaddicts, and former offenders. While the value of the program for youth and for exoffenders was negligible, exaddicts and, especially, AFDC recipients made impressive gains. The social rate of return for the AFDC group exceeded 100 percent. In other words, the benefit-cost ratio was well over two, a rate of return far exceeding the rate of return on a college education or on most types of tangible investment.

In recent years, "manpower programs" for the disadvantaged have gotten a bad name. In general, they have had overly ambitious and often conflicting objectives. They were sometimes poorly designed to achieve these objectives, and they were often poorly managed. The preceding examples demonstrate their potential effectiveness. Their image has been tarnished by an unwillingness in some quarters to separate the good from the bad or to admit that some programs have failed. But by the same token, there are success stories here upon which to build a firmer foundation for the future.

In the future there could be less commitment to programs for the disadvantaged because of a scarcity of funds and a belief that there are better ways to invest the federal training dollar. Shortages of engineers, scientists, and other technical personnel are creating bottlenecks for high-technology industries, and it is hardly realistic to assume one can train many high school dropouts or welfare mothers to become electrical engineers. Thus, relieving such shortages could necessitate a reallocation of existing federal training subsidies to technical education programs. There are three arguments which can be made against such a reallocation. The first is that we do not know for sure whether investments in training the more advantaged for high-skill occupations have higher payoffs for society than, say, making a low-income woman heading a family more economically independent. Second, assuming training for the more advantaged does have a higher payoff, equity considerations might still dictate preferential treatment for the most needy. Third, some (limited) incentives exist for state governments and large employers to provide training in skill-shortage occupations, but few profit-making organizations or local areas want to compete to provide services to, and thus become a haven for, the most disadvantaged. If this responsibility is not borne by the federal government, it may not be met at all.

Assisting Dislocated Workers—The argument for assisting dislocated workers is based on the possible hardship that plant shutdowns or layoffs may impose on individuals, their families and communities, and on the need to have a mechanism to induce workers to accept technological and other kinds of industrial change. In the absence of such a mechanism, there could be strong political pressures to bail out weak industries, to discourage imports, and to introduce more restrictive work practices or job protection schemes.

Past adjustment assistance efforts have been fragmented (there are some twenty-two different employee protection programs) and have emphasized cash benefits rather than retraining or other employment services. Under the largest of these programs (trade adjustment assistance), as much as 75 percent of the benefits has been paid to those who were temporarily laid off or put on short hours rather than to those suffering a permanent job loss. In short, trade adjustment assistance has been a form of extra generous unemployment insurance paid to just one group of workers, whose needs may be no greater than those of other unemployed workers.

The fact that past programs have been poorly designed is not an argument for ignoring the problem. The benefits of new technology and of a free trade economy are widely shared, but the costs are highly concentrated. This is the rationale for providing some form of worker adjustment assistance at public expense. Alternatively, the problem could be resolved within the private sector. Many union contracts call for employer-financed training, retraining programs, and provision of advance notice of layoffs or plant closings. If properly designed and administered, such programs need not be very expensive since the problem is not nearly as massive as many have assumed. According to an Urban Institute study by Marc Bendick and Judith R. Devine, dislocated workers —defined as those previously employed in declining industries who had been looking for work for at least eight weeks—in March

1980 numbered about 400,000 or about 6 percent of the 6.4 million unemployed at that time. They are typically semiskilled operatives who formerly worked in autos, textiles, steel, lumber, or other traditional manufacturing industries located in the Northeast and Midwest.

Upgrading the Skills of the Labor Force—It can be argued that as long as workers are free to move between employers and geographic areas, private firms and local governments will underinvest in education and training. In addition, the maturing of the baby boom, the entry of many adult women into the labor force, and the growth of new industries are likely to create the need for more adult training and retraining programs in the future. Finally, increasing levels of education and general affluence may make the labor force much more receptive to such opportunities and willing to share in the financing of them if mechanisms can be developed to make this possible. For example, some portion of payroll taxes might be earmarked for a "human resource investment account" which would entitle experienced workers to partake in a variety of on-the-job or classroom training activities throughout the life cycle. The federal government would need to provide leadership in developing such a plan and could contribute a portion of the funding. Alternatively, all of the financing could be provided by individuals and business firms.

Managing Human Resources

Human resources are both means and ends. As workers, individuals determine what can be produced. As consumers, they enjoy the fruits of that production. As members of social and political communities, they care about how work is organized and how income and status are distributed. Perceptions about the fairness and adequacy of the reward system, in turn, affect worker productivity.

By recognizing the human element in human resources and involving workers more in decision making, the Japanese are purported to have had more success than their western counterparts in motivating employees and sustaining rapid advances in labor productivity. (During the decade of the 1970s, labor productivity increased about twice as fast in Japan as in the U.S., although the *level* of U.S. productivity is still higher.) According to William Ouchi, the ingredients of the Japanese system include:

1. *Lifetime employment.* For the 35 percent of the work force in large companies and government offices, virtually all employees are hired upon school graduation and remain with the organization until age fifty-five. Under this arrangement, management has an incentive to invest in worker training, and employees care more about the success of the company.

2. *Slow evaluation and promotion.* Formal evaluation, promotion, and hierarchical distinctions of rank and salary are less important than peer group pressures in securing high levels of performance. Every worker is a member of a team or group which provides informal rewards and sanctions to its members.

3. *Nonspecialized career paths.* Employees typically learn many different jobs within the same organization and become company-oriented rather than skill-oriented over their careers.

4. *Implicit control mechanisms.* Because each employee knows what the general objectives, style, and philosophy of the organization are, there is less need for establishing explicit performance standards or targets.

5. *Collective responsibility.* The Japanese recognize that production requires a team effort and resist attempts to allocate credit or blame for results among individuals.

6. *Holistic concern for people.* Work life is not segregated from other aspects of life. There is greater socializing among employees and between workers and managers.

Although these six characteristics may reflect, and be particularly appropriate to, Japanese cultural traditions, Ouchi was able to identify a number of American companies with similar characteristics (IBM, Procter & Gamble, Hewlett-Packard, Eastman Kodak). He terms companies with this more democratic and employee-oriented management style "Type Z" organizations to be contrasted with the more conventional American or "Type A" organization. Within Type Z organizations there is sufficient socialization to the common goals of the organization that extrinsic rewards, close supervision, and bureaucratic rules are less necessary, according to Ouchi. However, he also points out that Type Z organizations have their weaknesses. They may be less innovative, be less open to new ideas, have a less "professional" staff, and be more culturally homogeneous—often excluding women, minorities, and others who are "different." In fact, many observers have gone further and suggested that the attributes of such organizations are in basic conflict with such American values as cultural diversity, independence, individualism, and privacy.

Whatever the merits of Type Z organizations, experimentation with new management styles including quality of work life (QWL) programs, quality circles, profit sharing, union representation on boards of directors, and other participative schemes are now very much in vogue in the United States.

According to Richard Walton, a professor at the Harvard Business School, experiments with these new techniques have been undertaken by a substantial minority of Fortune 500 companies, including such leaders as General Motors, Exxon, General Foods, TRW, Cummins Engine, Citibank, and Prudential Insurance. Unions, after initially being concerned that such schemes were an attempt to "get more out of the workers" without providing compensating rewards, have become somewhat more supportive in recent years.

Is this new enthusiasm for workplace innovations warranted or is it simply a fad? According to the advocates of more worker involvement in decision making, the benefits include less turnover and absenteeism, more satisfied and productive employees, and higher quality products. Rigorous evidence for these propositions is difficult to obtain, but studies by the Work in America Institute and others suggest that when programs are carefully implemented, the claims are justified. One of the most successful experiments, continuously cited in the literature, is General Motors's plant in Tarrytown, New York, which went from being one of the least productive of their plants in 1970 to one of the most productive in 1979. The union reports that absenteeism is down from around 7 percent to between 2 and 3 percent and that the number of grievances on file went from over 2,000 to 32.

Not all experiments have been similarly beneficial. According to Professor Walton, James O'Toole, and other experts, those most likely to succeed are those which entail top management commitment to produce fundamental and long-term changes and that give equal weight to improving employee satisfaction and rewards, on the one hand, and productivity and company performance, on the other. Based on the experience of about three dozen projects, Walton believes the average effectiveness of innovative work systems is higher than the average of more conventionally managed, but otherwise comparable, plants. However, he notes that there is a normal distribution of successes and failures around the average.

One way to give workers more of a stake in their enterprises and to secure their cooperation in improving productivity and product quality is through financial incentives, such as profit sharing, bonuses, and employee stock ownership plans. In Japan, workers receive semiannual bonuses, and these bonuses are linked to company profitability. An unintended, but potentially important, consequence of such "gain-sharing" systems is more flexible wages and prices and less unemployment. Currently, most of any reduction in overall demand—whether due to the normal workings of the business cycle or a conscious policy of monetary restraint aimed at curbing inflation—results in lower production and employment, rather than in more moderate wage and price rises. The more inflexible wages and prices are, the more painful and costly it is to use monetary restraint to reduce inflation. Under current institutional arrangements, it is estimated that the economic slack required to eliminate the double-digit inflation that existed in early 1980 would cost $1.2 trillion (an average of $15,000 per family) in lost production and income during the first half of the decade. By making wages and prices more flexible, the spread of compensation systems linking pay to economic performance could eliminate some of these costs.

To encourage such institutional reform, economist Daniel Mitchell has suggested that organizations be provided with tax incentives to introduce various forms of gain sharing that would make wages more sensitive to the health of the employer, the industry, or even the national economy. He argues that, unlike wage-price controls or other incomes policies, gain sharing is compatible with the existing system of decentralized collective bargaining and multiyear contracts in the United States. In addition to being tied to the cost-of-living through an escalator clause, under a gain-sharing system, wages would be automatically linked to an indicator of the overall economic health of the enterprise or the economy. Thus, institutional reforms affecting the way work is organized and rewarded have the potential to both improve productivity and the short-run trade-off between inflation and unemployment.

Conclusion

Reviving economic growth, reducing unemployment, and controlling inflation are high on the nation's agenda. There are a number of areas where improvements in the utilization, development, and management of human resources could contribute to these objectives.

First, barriers and disincentives to full participation in the labor force can reduce the proportion of the population that works. This not only creates a higher than necessary dependency ratio but may also require more taxes—which have their own disincentive effects—to support the dependent population. In terms of sheer numbers as well as sensitivity to public and private policies that encourage or discourage work, two groups stand out: adult women and older Americans. In particular, the Social Security System and institutional arrangements that make combining parenthood and work difficult bear scrutiny. Of course, the utilization of these groups will depend as much on the growth of demand as it does on incentives to work.

Second, the job opportunities of the future will be predominantly and increasingly in white-collar or service occupations. They will not necessarily require more people with college degrees —in fact, a glut of college-educated workers is currently forecast; however, good secondary school preparation seems essential. Recent declines in student performance at the high school level should be a cause for concern.

Third, fears that a new industrial revolution is going to produce widespread technological unemployment seem unjustified. The benefits of maintaining technological preeminence are many, and while this imposes severe costs on particular individuals and localities, in the aggregate these seem both modest and manageable through the use of appropriate adjustment assistance policies.

Fourth, although not all programs have been equally valuable, a continuing federal commitment to assist the disadvantaged to become more economically independent seems like a worthwhile investment of federal funds.

Fifth, federal leadership in assuring the availability of privately financed mid-career training opportunities may be desirable; the case for federal subsidies is less compelling.

Finally, more innovative ways of managing and rewarding workers have considerable potential to improve productivity, humanize work, and make fighting inflation less painful.

Edwin Mansfield

6

Science and Technology

Introduction

My task in this chapter is to discuss the role that science and technology will play in determining the state of the American economy in the year 2000, and the major issues regarding our nation's technology policies that are likely to arise during the period up to the end of this century. Obviously, this is a very broad topic. For this chapter to be of reasonable length, it must be highly selective. After defining what is meant by technological change and innovation and indicating the importance of technological change in the process of economic growth, I shall describe very briefly some of the advances in biotechnology, information technology, and electronics that, in the opinion of leading technolo-

EDWIN MANSFIELD *is professor of economics at the University of Pennsylvania, having previously taught at Carnegie-Mellon, Yale, Harvard, and the California Institute of Technology. Dr. Mansfield has been a consultant to many public agencies and has served on advisory committees for the President's Domestic Policy Review of Industrial Innovation, the National Science Foundation, and the Bureau of the Census. In 1979 'he was the first U.S. economist invited by the People's Republic of China to lecture there. In addition to publishing over 135 articles, he is the author of nineteen books, the most recent being* Technology Transfer, Productivity, and Economic Policy, *which contains a much more detailed treatment of the topics discussed in this chapter.*

gists, are likely to have important future effects. Then I shall discuss the alleged slowdown in the U.S. rate of innovation, some possible reasons for such a slowdown, and the relevant public policy issues that are likely to come to the fore in the next decade or two. Next, I shall describe very briefly the decline in the U.S. technological lead over its trading partners, and the prospects in this area, after which a few words are said about the problems that are likely to arise in adjusting to technological change in the 1980s and 1990s.

Science, Technology, and Innovation

To begin with, it is essential to define such terms as science, technology, and innovation. Technology consists of society's pool of knowledge concerning the industrial, agricultural, and medical arts. It is made up of knowledge concerning physical and social phenomena, knowledge regarding the application of basic principles to practical work, and knowledge of the rules of thumb of practitioners and craftsmen. Although the distinction between science and technology is imprecise, it is important. Science is aimed at understanding, whereas technology is aimed at use. Changes in technology often take place as a consequence of inventions that depend on no new scientific principles. Indeed, until the middle of the nineteenth century, there was only a loose connection between science and technology. However, in recent years, technology has come to be much more closely intertwined with science.

A technological innovation is defined as the first commercial introduction of new technology. Research and development (R and D) is only a part of the process leading to a successful technological innovation. The first part of this process takes place in the interval between the establishment of technical feasibility and the beginning of commercial development of the new product or process. This time interval may be substantial (although it is shorter now than fifty years ago). For example, it often was about a decade for important postwar innovations, like numerical control, freeze-dried food, and integrated circuits. The second part of this process takes place in the time interval between the beginning of commercial development and the first commercial application of the new process or product. This time interval contains a number of distinct stages—applied research, preparation of product specification, prototype or pilot plant construction, tooling and construction of manufacturing facilities, and manufacturing and marketing start-up. In all, this time interval has often been about five years for important postwar innovations.

Technological Change and Economic Growth

The fundamental and widespread effects of technological change are obvious. Technological change has permitted the reduction of working hours, improved working conditions, provided a wide variety of extraordinary new products, increased the flow of old products, and added a great many dimensions to the life of our citizens. At the same time, technological change also has its darker side. Advances in military technology have enabled modern nation-states to cause human destruction on an unprecedented scale, modern technology has contributed to various kinds of air and water pollution, and advances in industrial technology have sometimes resulted in widespread unemployment in particular occupations and communities. Despite the many benefits that society has reaped from technological change, no one would regard it as an unalloyed blessing.

The fact that technological change plays an important role in permitting and stimulating the growth of per capita output seems self-evident. But when one wants to go beyond such bland generalizations to a quantitative summary of the contribution of technological change to the rate of economic growth, a number of basic difficulties are encountered. For one thing, it is hard to separate the effects on economic growth of technological change from those of investment in physical capital, since, to be used, new technology frequently must be embodied in physical capital —new machines and plant. For example, a numerically controlled machine tool (or control mechanism) must be built to take full advantage of some of the advances in the technology related to machine tools. Nor can the effects of technological change easily be separated from those of education, since the social returns from increased education are enhanced by technological change, and the rate of technological change is influenced by the extent and nature of society's investment in education.

Despite these and other problems, economists have tried to obtain quantitative measures of the importance of technological change in American economic growth. For example, Edward Denison has estimated that the advance of knowledge was responsible for about 40 percent of the total increase in national income per person employed during 1929–1957 in the United States. Although studies of this sort have an impressive number of limitations, most economists believe that they demonstrate beyond any reasonable doubt that technological change is one of the principle factors, perhaps the most important factor, determining a nation's rate of economic growth.

Technological Advance: Biotechnology

Having indicated what is meant by science, technology, and innovation and having described the contribution of technological change to economic growth, it is appropriate to discuss some of the innovations, and changes in technology, that are likely to occur and/or spread before the year 2000. I shall concentrate on biotechnology, information technology, and electronics, since they are some of the most dynamic and promising areas of technology at present.

It is well known that spectacular advances have been made in biotechnology in recent years. The development of recombinant DNA techniques was a milestone in the history of science. These techniques involved the employment of restriction enzymes to isolate and remove gene sequences from DNA molecules and to recombine them with the DNA of other organisms. Also involved was the application of methods to reproduce large amounts of exact copies (clones) of the hybrid or recombinant DNA molecules.

According to the National Research Council, in *Outlook for Science and Technology: The Next Five Years* (1981):

Recombinant DNA technology in theory should permit any protein or small set of proteins to be made in convenient hosts. Organisms perform an almost infinite variety of chemical conversions by means of enzymes (protein catalysts); the genes that specify the synthesis of the desired enzymes could be recombined and used to produce the enzymes. The limiting factors are the ability to isolate the particular gene and to arrange matters so that it functions efficiently in a host that replicates well in an inexpensive medium.

Most observers seem to believe that the first commercial products to be made from recombinant DNA technology almost certainly will be drugs. Insulin, growth hormone, and interferon seem to be among those that are particularly close to large-scale production. Chemical firms seem to be interested in using the technology to make products like acetone, butyl alcohol, and ethyl alcohol. Also, food processing and agriculture may be areas where recombinant DNA technology may find major applications.

Since the industrial applications of biotechnology are so new, it is very difficult to predict how extensive or important they will be by the year 2000. Some experts believe that there will eventually be a great impact on agriculture. By using techniques like gene splicing and cloning, researchers are trying to develop types of plants that can survive in harsh environments. Also, attempts are being made to develop new types of crops that are resistant to particular herbicides.

Work is also going on to modify the genetics of animals. Research workers are trying to produce livestock more resistant to disease and capable of increased yields of meat or milk. There is talk of developing new species of animals, and in fact scientists have succeeded in implanting genes from a rabbit into a mouse. How far and how fast this work will proceed is impossible to predict. Even the most enthusiastic practitioners of technological forecasting admit that it is not a well-developed science. All that can be said is that the potential effects on the economy seem to be substantial.

One important factor that may influence the rate and direction of development of the young biotechnology industry is the debate over safety. Some observers fear the possible effects of a continued accumulation of new substances resulting from DNA research. Others worry about careless laboratory practices. Industry spokespersons retort that the risks are greatly exaggerated. Most, if not all, companies have announced that they would comply with federal guidelines. Nonetheless, cities and towns in Massachusetts, such as Cambridge, Boston, and Newton, have begun writing regulations for the industry.

Technological Advance: Information Technology and Electronics

In information technology, there have been enormous advances. Information and data processing technologies are associated largely with computers. According to experts in the field, the cost of computer main memory has been going down by 26 percent per year since 1965 and is expected to continue to do so through the 1980s. To cite a couple of other examples illustrating the nature of recent developments, there are (1) commercially available storage technologies that permit access times as low as one-billionth of a second for storage used to process information and (2) videodisks that can store as many as 10 billion bits of information on a disk that is the size of a phonograph record.

The telephone has been changed from a signal transport device into a message processor capable of carrying out a variety of tasks. Digital data networks have augmented access to on-line information retrieval systems. As pointed out in a recent report by an American Association for the Advancement of Science committee:

> Facsimile transmission is widespread. Optical fibers can carry more simultaneous messages than conventional cable. Cable television has enormous potential for home information services, and videodisks and videocassette recorders could have a substantial impact on education as well as home entertainment. The publishing industry is being changed by the transmission of news and literature via telecommunications and broadcasting systems. Communication satellites provide the means for inexpensive, reliable, and real-time information transfer on a global scale.

In addition, the so-called "office of the future" is beginning to take shape. According to Donald Hillman, in *Science, Technology, and the Issues of the Eighties: Policy Outlook:*

> Future office managers will be able not only to create local communications networks but also to transmit large amounts of information over great distances. They will use the newly developed computer-generated graphics to display financial and operational data needed for management reporting

and strategic analysis and thereby enhance their ability for informed decision making.

Microelectronics has seen very great advances. The capability of silicon integrated circuits has grown, with commensurate improvements in cost and reliability. According to the National Research Council, the dimensions of circuit elements have been cut to the point where existing knowledge of materials properties is inadequate and more research is needed. The increase in the capabilities of integrated circuits has been particularly rapid in logic and memory circuits. Electronics firms now put as many of these circuits into a single chip of silicon as were employed in total to construct the early vacuum tube computers. Among other things, this has led to the increased use of digital electronics in communications and computer technologies.

Microprocessors are used more and more in industrial process control. Important advances are also being made in computer-aided design (CAD) and computer-aided manufacturing (CAM), used together. The CAD/CAM automated factory has been described by J. Scrimgeour in "An Overview of CAD/CAM in Canada Today" (*Canadian Datasystems,* October 1979) as follows:

> Computer graphics for the design and drafting of the product, with the design held in computer memory rather than by drawings and blueprints, computer-generated parts lists, vendor ordering, production scheduling and inventory control . . . computer-controlled stacking cranes for automatic movement of material, assembly areas employing robotics and direct computer control of numerically controlled machine tools, inspection and automatic test equipment.

Turning from the factory to the service sector of the economy, new electronics technologies are being widely diffused. Point of sale terminals, optical character recognition for inventory control, and automated warehousing are being adopted. Financial institutions are using electronic fund transfer systems and automated methods of handling paper-based transactions. Word processors and other types of equipment are penetrating the office. Pocket calculators, electronic watches, and T.V. games have entered the home. And many consumer durable goods are being altered by the new electronics technologies. For example, sewing machines, washing machines, ovens, and automobiles are some examples of familiar products in and around the home that now include microprocessors, both to replace older electromechanical components and sometimes to perform new functions.

The 1980s and 1990s will see a continuation of these trends toward a greater utilization of electronic devices. According to a report issued by the Organization for Economic Cooperation and Development, *Technological Change and Economic Policy: The Electronic Industry:*

> The recent and ongoing wave of rapid innovation in the electronics sector has been underpinned by the technical change in a limited range of basic technologies (mostly silicone-based) in the components sector. The development of these *basic* technologies is near the [point where diminishing gains in performance are likely to be achieved] . . . whereas the rate of innovation in devices and equipment (except, perhaps, in the consumer goods subsector) *derived* from these technologies is at the . . . [point where gains in performance are likely to be very high].

Slowdown in the Rate of Technological Innovation?

Based on the previous two sections, the rate of innovation in the United States is likely to be high in the 1980s and 1990s. But biotechnology, information technology, and electronics are not typical areas of technology. If one looks at the entire range of technology, there is some evidence that the rate of technological innovation may be slowing down. This evidence is of three types.

1. The U.S. rate of productivity increase slowed down notably since the mid–1960s, the drop being particularly great since the mid–1970s. According to the Council of Economic Advisers, output per hour of labor increased by 1 percent during 1973–1977, as compared with 2.3 percent during 1965–1973. Between 1977 and 1978, it increased by less than 1 percent. And based on indexes prepared by the Bureau of Labor Statistics, output per hour of labor in the private business sector did not increase at all from 1978 to 1980. Of course, the fact that there has been a productivity slowdown does not prove by itself that there has been a slowdown in the rate of innovation. But many experts, such as John Kendrick, believe that the productivity slowdown is due in part to a reduction in the rate of innovation.

2. The patent rate in the United States has been falling since

about 1969. In practically all of the fifty-two product fields for which data are available, the number of patents granted annually (by year of application) to U.S. inventors declined during the 1970s (Table 1). However, the crudeness of patent statistics as a

TABLE 1. U.S. PATENTS GRANTED TO U.S. INVENTORS, BY YEAR OF APPLICATION, 1965–1976

Year	Number of Patents (in thousands)	Year	Number of Patents (in thousands)
1965	42.2	1971	45.5
1966	45.0	1972	42.4
1967	44.2	1973	42.6
1968	45.3	1974	41.6
1969	46.4	1975	41.7
1970	45.8	1976	40.2

Source: Based on information from *Science Indicators, 1980* (Washington, D.C.: National Science Foundation, 1981).

measure of the rate of innovation should be emphasized. The average importance of the patents granted at one time and place may differ from those granted at another time and place. The proportion of total inventions that are patented may vary significantly. Nonetheless, for what it is worth, there has been a decline in the patent rate (both in other countries, like West Germany, France, and the United Kingdom, as well as in the United States), and it often is viewed as evidence of a decline in the rate of innovation.

3. In some industries where one can measure the number of major innovations carried out per unit of time, there seems to be direct evidence of a fall in the rate of innovations. For example, in the pharmaceutical industry, the number of new chemical entities introduced per year in the United States has declined relative to the 1950s and early 1960s. This measure suffers from the fact that it is difficult to find suitable weights for different innovations. Also, this measure overlooks the small innovations which sometimes have a bigger cumulative effect than some of the more spectacular innovations.

R and D Expenditures and the Rate of Innovation

Although it would be a mistake to regard the above statistics as reasonably reliable measures of the rate of innovation, it may well be that there has been some fall in the rate of innovation, particularly in areas like pharmaceuticals and agricultural chemicals, but not in areas like microelectronics or biotechnology. There are a number of reasons why such a slowdown might have been expected in recent years. The nation's total R and D expenditures, when inflation is taken roughly into account, seemed to remain essentially constant from 1967 to 1977 (Table 2). According to a considerable number of econometric studies, the rate of innovation is directly related to the rate of increase of R and D "capital," defined as the sum of previous (depreciated) R and D expenditures. Thus, the reduction during the 1960s and 1970s in the rate of growth of R and D expenditures would be expected to result in a reduction in the rate of innovation.

TABLE 2.   TOTAL EXPENDITURES FOR RESEARCH AND DEVELOPMENT, UNITED STATES, 1960–1980

Year	R and D Expenditures (Billions of 1972 Dollars)	Year	R and D Expenditures (Billions of 1972 Dollars)
1960	19.6	1971	27.8
1961	20.6	1972	28.4
1962	21.8	1973	29.1
1963	23.7	1974	28.8
1964	25.9	1975	28.2
1965	26.9	1976	29.5
1966	28.4	1977	30.7
1967	29.2	1978	32.0
1968	29.8	1979	33.3
1969	29.6	1980*	34.5
1970	28.5		

* Estimate by National Science Foundation.

Source: Based on information from Science Indicators, 1980 (Washington, D.C.: National Science Foundation, 1981).

What was responsible for the lack of growth of deflated R and D expenditures in the late 1960s and 1970s? There was a cut in government-financed R and D expenditures due in considerable measure to the winding down of the space program and to reduced defense programs. The reasons for the slowdown in the growth of industry's real R and D expenditures are less obvious, but the available evidence indicates that the private rate of return from investments in R and D was lower during the later 1960s and 1970s than during earlier periods. My own studies indicate this to be the case, based on econometric estimates and on a detailed study of the R and D portfolio of one of the nation's largest firms. To some extent, this reduction in the private rate of return may have been due to diminishing returns as more and more money was invested in R and D. To some extent, it may also have been due to increased regulatory requirements and other factors.

In addition to the fall in the rate of growth of R and D "capital," there has been a notable shift away from more basic, long-term, and risky R and D projects in many industries, such as aerospace, chemicals, and rubber. In metals, aerospace, drugs, glass, rubber, machinery, and chemicals, there was a significant reduction between 1967 and 1977 in the proportion of R and D expenditures aimed at entirely new products and processes, rather than at product and process improvements. It would be surprising if this change in the composition of R and D expenditures were not to depress the rate of innovation. In this connection, it is interesting to note that in electronics (where, as noted above, there is no clearcut evidence of a slowdown in the rate of innovation) there seems to have been no such reduction in the proportion of R and D expenditures going for long-term, risky, and ambitious projects.

What caused this change in the composition of R and D expenditures in many industries? Several reasons are given by R and D executives. The reason most frequently given (particularly in the drugs and chemical industries) was the increase in government regulations, which in their opinion reduced the profitability of relatively fundamental and risky projects. Another reason was that breakthroughs were more difficult to achieve than in the past, because the field has been more thoroughly worked over. Another reason was the high inflation rates in the 1970s, which will be discussed further below. Still another reason is that many firms have changed their view of how R and D should be managed. In the 1950s and early 1960s, firms frequently did not try to manage R and D in much detail. Subsequently, many firms began to emphasize control, formality in R and D project selection, and short-term effects on profit. This has tended to reduce the proportion of R and D expenditures going for basic and risky projects.

Is There an Underinvestment in Civilian Technology?

As pointed out in the previous section, the rate of innovation in the United States seems to be closely related to how much the nation's firms, universities, and government spend on R and D. According to many economists, there tends to be an underinvestment in R and D, particularly of more basic and long-term sorts.

What is the evidence that such an underinvestment exists? To begin with, it is generally agreed that because it is often difficult for firms to appropriate the benefits that society receives from new technology, there may be a tendency for too few resources to be devoted to the development of new civilian technology. It is also generally agreed that the extent to which these benefits are appropriable is probably related to the extent of competition faced by the firm and to the kind of research or development activity in question. In particular, the more competition there is and the more basic the work, the less appropriable it is likely to be.

Also, because R and D is a relatively risky activity, there may be a tendency for firms to invest too little in it, given that many firms seem to be averse to risk and that there are only limited and imperfect ways to shift risk. Further, some kinds of R and D may be characterized by significant economies of scale that prevent small organizations from undertaking them efficiently. It is often argued that some industries are so fragmented that they cannot do a proper amount of R and D.

While the preceding arguments have a considerable amount of force, they by no means prove that there is an underinvestment in civilian technology. For one thing, these arguments generally are based on the supposition that markets are perfectly competitive, whereas in fact many important markets are oligopolistic. For another thing, the government is intervening in a variety of ways to support civilian technology, and its actions may have offset whatever latent underinvestment in R and D was present in particular parts of the economy.

Since economists cannot rely solely on a priori theorizing to tell them whether there is an underinvestment in R and D in civilian technology (and if so, where it is most severe), they have turned to empirical studies of the returns from investment in civilian technology. These studies provide information concerning what society has received from various forms of R and D investments in the past. Of course, there is a variety of problems in measuring the social benefits from new technology. Any innovation, particularly a major one, has effects on many firms and industries, and it obviously is hard to evaluate each one and sum them up properly. Nonetheless, economists have devised techniques that should provide at least rough estimates of the social rate of return (that is, the rate of return to society as a whole) from particular innovations.

Practically all of the studies carried out to date indicate that the social rate of return from investments in new civilian technology has tended, on the average, to be very high. More important for present purposes, the marginal social rate of return—that is, the rate of return from the last dollar spent on developing and introducing new civilian technology—tends to be high, generally in the neighborhood of 30 to 50 percent. Such results suggest that there may be an underinvestment in civilian R and D. Of course, there is a variety of very important problems and limitations inherent in each of these studies, and they should be viewed with caution. But recognizing this fact, it is remarkable that so many independent studies based on such different data come to such similar conclusions.

Public Policies toward Civilian Technology

During the 1980s and 1990s, I believe that the following fundamental question will come increasingly to the fore: what policies, if any, should the federal government adopt to encourage industrial innovation? As pointed out in the previous section, there is considerable evidence that, from an economic point of view, the United States may be underinvesting in civilian technology. What steps should be taken to remedy the situation? It is not easy to provide answers that are both economically sensible and politically viable, but it is of the utmost importance that a sustained and continuing effort be made to find the best answers possible.

There is a variety of ways that the government might stimulate additional R and D in the private sector—tax credits, R and D contracts and grants, expanded work in government laboratories, loan insurance for innovation, purchasing policies with greater emphasis on performance criteria and life cycle costing, altered regulatory policies, and prizes. An important problem with a general tax credit is its inefficiency; an important advantage is that it involves less direct government controls. An important problem with more selective support mechanisms is that it is so difficult to estimate in advance the social benefits and costs of particular types of R and D projects. If a program of this sort were started, a combination of selective and more general forms of support would probably be most effective.

Although many economists suspect that there may be an underinvestment in certain areas of civilian technology, there is at the same time some concern that the federal government, in trying to improve matters, could do more harm than good. In this regard, the following five guidelines may be of use.

1. To the extent that such a program were selective, it should be neither large scale nor organized on a crash basis. Instead, it should be characterized by flexibility, small-scale probes, and parallel approaches. In view of the relatively small amount of information that is available and the great uncertainties involved, it should be organized, at least in part, to provide information concerning the returns from a larger program. On the basis of the information that results, a more informed judgment can be made concerning the desirability of increased or, for that matter, perhaps decreased amounts of support.

2. Any temptation to focus such a program on economically beleaguered industries should be rejected. The fact that an industry is in trouble or that it is declining or that it has difficulty competing with foreign firms is, by itself, no justification for additional R and D. More R and D may not have much payoff somewhere else in the economy. It is important to recall the circumstances under which the government is justified in augmenting private R and D. Practically all economists would agree that such aug-

mentation is justifiable if the private costs and benefits derived from R and D do not adequately reflect the social costs and benefits. But in many industries there is little or no evidence of a serious discrepancy of this sort between private and social costs and benefits. Indeed, some industries may spend too much, from society's point of view, on R and D.

3. Except in the most unusual circumstances, the government should avoid getting involved in the latter stages of development work. In general, this is an area where firms are far more adept than government agencies. Government programs in support of civilian technology should proceed on an incremental, step-by-step basis, to resolve scientific and technical uncertainties to the point where private firms can use the resulting information to decide when and how (with their own money) to move into full-scale commercial development. Although there may be cases where development costs are so high that private industry cannot obtain the necessary resources, or where it is so important to our national security or well-being that a particular technology be developed that the government must step in, these cases do not arise very often. Instead, the available evidence seems to indicate that when governments become involved in what is essentially commercial development, they are not very successful at it.

4. In any selective government program to increase support for civilian technology, it is vitally important that a proper coupling occur between technology and the market. Recent studies of industrial innovations point repeatedly to the key importance of this coupling. In choosing areas and projects for support, the government should be sensitive to market demand. To the extent that it is feasible, potential users of new technology should play a role in project selection. Information transfer and communication between the generators of new technology and the potential users of new technology are essential if new technology is to be successfully applied. As evidence of their importance, studies show that a sound coupling of technology and marketing is one of the characteristics that is most significant in distinguishing firms that are relatively successful innovators from those that are relatively unsuccessful innovators.

5. In formulating any such program, it is important to recognize the advantages of pluralism and decentralized decision mak-

ing. If the experience of the last twenty-five years in defense R and D elsewhere has taught us anything, it has taught us how difficult it is to plan technological development. Technological change, particularly of a major or radical sort, is marked by great uncertainty. It is difficult to predict which of a number of alternative projects will turn out best. Very important concepts and ideas come from unexpected sources. It would be a mistake for a program of this sort to rely too heavily on centralized planning. Moreover, it would be a mistake if the government attempted to carry out work that private industry can do better or more efficiently.

Importance of Macroeconomic Policies

In formulating policies regarding civilian technology, it is important to recognize that our nation's technology policies cannot be separated from its economic policies. Measures which encourage economic growth, saving and investment, and price stability are likely to enhance our technological position. Just as many of our current technological problems can be traced to sources outside science and engineering, so these problems may be resolved in considerable part by improvements in the general economic climate in the United States. Indeed, improvements in our general economic climate may have more impact on the state of U.S. technology than many of the specific measures that have been proposed to stimulate technical change.

To illustrate how the general economic climate influences technological change, consider the effects on the high rates of inflation that the United States has experienced in recent years. Inflation that is high on the average tends to be very variable in its rate, and this reduces the efficiency of the price system as a mechanism for coordinating economic activity. In particular, both liberal and conservative economists stress that high rates of inflation often have serious negative effects on investment.

In addition, R and D is affected as well. By themselves, research and development frequently are of little value to a firm. Only when they are combined with plant and equipment and with manufacturing, marketing, and financial capabilities do they result in a commercially meaningful new product or process. To the extent that inflation reduces investment rates, it tends to discourage the sort of R and D that requires new plant and equipment for its utilization. To the extent that inflation makes long-run prediction of prices and circumstances increasingly hazardous, it tends to discourage the sorts of R and D that are long-term and relatively ambitious. Indeed, many of the reasons why inflation adversely affects investment in plant and equipment hold equally well for investment in relatively ambitious R and D projects. This does not mean that firms necessarily cut back on their R and D expenditures in inflationary times. But there are indications that they often are less inclined to fund long-term and relatively ambitious R and D projects than would be the case under a regime of relative price stability.

High rates of inflation can also have a negative impact on government financed R and D. Faced with excessive inflation, governments may feel compelled to trim R and D budgets as part of an antiinflationary fiscal policy. To the extent that this R and D would promote more rapid productivity increase in the long run, this may have the unintended effect of lowering productivity growth and perhaps worsening inflation then.

To prevent misunderstanding, it must be added that very high unemployment rates, as well as very high inflation rates, will tend to discourage innovation. When sales are depressed and the future looks grim, the climate for innovation is hardly bright. Neither severe and prolonged recession nor double-digit inflation constitute a benign climate for industrial innovation. I have focused attention on inflation only because its effects tend to be more subtle than those of severe unemployment.

Technological Innovation and U.S. Competitiveness in World Markets

Besides being an important determinant of our nation's rate of economic growth, the rate and direction of technological innovation influence how competitive American firms are in world markets. Although economists have been aware for over a century that technological change is one determinant of the nature and size of a country's imports and exports, there has been increasing emphasis on this factor in the past ten or fifteen years. Both from case studies and statistical analyses, economists have found that U.S. industries that spend relatively large amounts on R and D are the ones that lead in manufactured exports, foreign direct investment, and licensing. Needless to say, there is an enormous amount that remains to be learned concerning the relationship between technological change and our foreign trade. But the available evidence seems to suggest that technological innovation has had a major influence on American exports, receipts from licenses, and direct investment abroad.

In many areas where we have a favorable balance of trade, our comparative advantage seems to be based on a technological edge. In R and D–intensive manufacturing industries, such as machinery, aircraft, chemicals, and instruments, the United States has maintained a favorable balance of trade for many years. On the other hand, in non–R and D–intensive manufacturing industries, the United States has experienced a very large negative trade balance in the past decade. Of course, many factors—such as exchange rates, tariffs, quotas, and the aggressiveness and effectiveness with which firms try to market their products abroad—influence our trade position. But there seems to be widespread agreement among economists and others that the role of technology in U.S. foreign trade is important.

The available evidence suggests that the United States long has been a leader in technology. Even before 1850, there is scattered evidence of such a technology gap. After 1850, total factor productivity was higher in the United States than in Europe, the United States had a strong export position in technically dynamic industries, and Europeans tended to imitate American methods. Naturally, the United States did not lead in all fields, but it appears that we held a technological lead in many important areas of manufacturing. The existence of such a technology gap in the nineteenth century is not surprising, since this was a golden era of American invention—the days of Thomas Edison, Robert Fulton, Samuel Morse, Cyrus McCormick, and many others.

Due in part to the wartime devastation of many countries in Europe and Asia, there was a widespread feeling that the U.S. technological lead widened after World War II. In the 1960s, Europeans expressed considerable concern over the technology gap. They asserted that superior know-how stemming from scientific and technological achievements in the United States had permitted American firms to obtain large shares of European markets in industries like aircraft, space equipment, computers, and other electronic products. In 1966, Italy's Foreign Minister Amintore Fanfani went so far as to call for a "technological Marshall Plan" to speed the flow of U.S. technology across the Atlantic.

The Reduction of the U.S. Technological Lead

During the past fifteen or twenty years, the U.S. technological lead has been reduced in many areas, and in some areas it no longer exists at all. This is the judgment of many leading engineers, scientists, and managers, both here and abroad. Unfortunately, it is extremely difficult to measure international gaps in technology levels, but at least three types of evidence seem to be consistent with this view.

1. Productivity has increased much more slowly in the United States than in Western Europe and Japan. Between 1960 and 1980, output per hour of labor increased by 184 percent in France, 174 percent in West Germany, 465 percent in Japan, 79 percent in the United Kingdom, and 69 percent in the United States (Table 3). To some extent, our relatively poor rate of productivity increase has been due to a relatively low rate of increase of plant and equipment. But this is only part of the story. Total factor

TABLE 3. GROWTH IN OUTPUT PER HOUR, MANUFACTURING INDUSTRIES, SELECTED COUNTRIES, 1960–1980

(1977 = 100)

Year	United States	France	West Germany	Japan	United Kingdom	Soviet Union
1960	60.1	40.0	40.0	21.7	58.3	55.9
1965	74.6	51.5	53.5	32.8	69.9	66.6
1970	79.2	70.6	68.5	60.7	83.2	77.6
1975	93.5	88.4	89.3	84.0	95.0	96.3
1980	101.4	113.4	109.5	122.7	104.4	NA

Source: Based on information from *Science Indicators, 1980* (Washington, D.C.: National Science Foundation, 1981).

productivity (which takes account of both labor and capital inputs) seems to have risen relatively slowly in the United States. Although it is difficult to determine how much of this is due to a narrowing of our technological lead, it is reasonable to believe that it is one of the reasons.

2. The National Science Foundation has published the results of a study which indicate that the United States originated about 80 percent of the major innovations in 1953–1958, about 67 percent of the major innovations in 1959–1964, and about 57 percent of the major innovations in 1965–1973. Without more information concerning the way in which the sample of innovations was drawn, it is difficult to tell whether the apparent reduction in the proportion of industrial innovations stemming from the U.S. is due to the sampling procedures. Also, without some weighting of the innovations, these data are difficult to interpret. But taken at face value, the findings suggest a reduction in America's technological lead.

3. While R and D expenditures have decreased as a percentage of gross national product in the United States during 1967–1979,

TABLE 4. RESEARCH AND DEVELOPMENT EXPENDITURES AS PERCENTAGE OF GROSS NATIONAL PRODUCT, SELECTED COUNTRIES, 1962–1980

Year	United States	France	West Germany	Japan	United Kingdom	Soviet Union
			Total R and D Expenditures as Percentage of GNP			
1962	2.73	1.46	1.25	1.47	NA	2.64
1967	2.89	2.13	1.97	1.53	2.30	2.91
1972	2.40	1.86	2.33	1.85	2.06	3.58
1977	2.24	1.77	2.32	1.92	NA	3.46
1980	2.33	NA	NA	NA	NA	3.47
			Civilian R and D Expenditures as Percentage of GNP			
1962	1.23	1.03	1.14	1.46	NA	NA
1967	1.48	1.50	1.70	1.52	1.65	NA
1972	1.44	1.35	2.13	1.81	1.48	NA
1977	1.52	1.38	2.14	1.87	NA	NA
1980	1.63	NA	NA	NA	NA	NA

Source: Based on information from *Science Indicators, 1980* (Washington, D.C.: National Science Foundation, 1981).

they have increased in other countries, such as Japan, West Germany, and the Soviet Union (Table 4). At this point, based on official figures, the percentage of GNP devoted to R and D is higher in West Germany and the Soviet Union than in the United States. Moreover, it is important to point out that the United States allocates a substantial amount of its R and D spending to defense and space programs. Although defense and space R and D can have important "spillover" effects on civilian technology, their effects are unlikely to be as great, dollar for dollar, as R and D aimed directly at civilian technology. Looking only at civilian R and D expenditures, it appears that both West Germany and Japan devote a larger share of their GNP to such expenditures than does the United States (Table 4).

However, this evidence should be treated with caution. R and D expenditures are a measure of input into the innovation process, not output. Moreover, they are a very incomplete measure of input, since much more than R and D is required to introduce a new product or process. Further, it is doubtful whether the data for countries like the Soviet Union are comparable with those for the United States. Also, a considerable portion of the industrial R and D in some major foreign countries, notably Canada, West Germany, and the United Kingdom, is done by U.S.–based multinational firms. And more basically, a nation's competitiveness depends on how effectively it uses both foreign and domestic technology, and this may not be measured at all well by its ratio of R and D spending to gross national product.

U.S. Technology: Status and Prospects

Although our technological lead seems to have been reduced in many industries, U.S. technology continues to be generally very strong. One measure of this strength is the amount we earn from the sale of technical know-how. In 1978, the U.S. received about $5.4 billion and paid foreigners less than $0.7 billion in royalties and fees. As is well known, these figures must be treated with caution because they are influenced by tax and other considerations. But nevertheless it seems fair to say that while the U.S. does not have the commanding lead it enjoyed twenty years ago, its technology is strong indeed.

Nonetheless, the prospect over the coming decades is for increased international rivalry in many key technological areas. In electronics, for example, Japan has established a national program to accelerate its technological activities. The Japanese have made great strides in microelectronics. For example, they won a major victory in the market for the 64K RAM, where they were reported to have 70 to 80 percent of the market in 1982. According to a report to Congress in 1981 by the National Research Council, the work in the Japanese nationally supported effort "appears to have gone far beyond anything done in the United States outside IBM and Bell Laboratories."

In chemicals, there are large, aggressive firms in Western Europe and Japan that are carrying out major R and D programs. For example, West Germany's Big Three—BASF, Bayer, and Hoechst—each spend about $0.5 billion or more a year on R and D. According to the National Research Council:

> The major European companies are spending higher percentages of their sales dollars on R and D than are American firms and are focusing on the same areas of research. While they have the same problems of rising fuelstock costs, they nevertheless appear to be building a technological base that could well make them a dominant force in world markets by the 1980s.

In pharmaceuticals, where Swiss, German, and other non–U.S.–based multinational firms have long held major positions, the Japanese are becoming increasingly important. According to a recent study, the top forty-nine multinational drug companies break down as follows: twenty-two United States, ten Japanese, seven West German, four British, three Swiss, two French, and one Italian. During 1975–1978, world-wide sales of the ten Japanese firms were reported to have increased from 30 to 60 percent per year per company. As the National Research Council says, "A continuation of this trend could have a significant impact on the future of the U.S.–based pharmaceutical industry."

Besides being the focus of more intense international rivalry, technology is also likely to become increasingly internationalized in coming decades. This tendency has already manifested itself in many industries. For example, in the pharmaceutical industry, often it no longer is true that a new drug is discovered, tested, and commercialized, all within a single country. Instead, the discovery phase of a project frequently involves collaboration among laboratories and researchers located in several different countries, even when they are within the same firm. And clinical testing generally becomes a multicountry project. Even in the latter stages of drug development, such as dosage formulation, work often is done in more than one country. In more and more cases, it no longer is true that an innovation is carried out in a single country or that the technology resides exclusively within that country for a considerable period after the innovation's initial commercial introduction.

Adjusting to Technological Change

Before concluding, it should be stressed once more that technological change is not an unalloyed blessing. Society, which is, by and large, a beneficiary of technological change, has tried in various ways to assist the readjustment of those who are hurt by it. But many problems remain. In the next couple of decades, these problems will continue to be important.

With regard to the effects of technological change on workers, the first thing to be said is that rapid technological change need not result in increases in aggregate unemployment. Changes in aggregate unemployment are governed by the growth in the aggregate demand for goods and services and the growth in the labor force, as well as the growth in output per man-hour. If the rate of increase of aggregate demand equals the rate of increase of productivity plus the rate of increase of the labor force, there will be no increase in aggregate unemployment, no matter how high the rate of productivity may be. Although there will be increases in some types of jobs and decreases in others, the total number of unemployed will not be affected.

But this does not mean that labor will not have to move from one occupation, industry, or region to another. Nor would we want to eliminate such movements of labor, without which it would be impossible to adjust to changes in technology, population, and consumer tastes. However, regardless of the long-run benefits of this adjustment process, important problems may arise in the short run, great distress being imposed on the workers who are displaced. It is important that these movements of labor be carried out as efficiently and painlessly as possible.

There seems to be general agreement that, if possible, reductions in employment due to the adoption of new techniques (and other forms of change) should be carried out by attrition—retirements and voluntary quits. Also, it is often recommended that advance notice be given by employers of the possibility or inevitability of major layoffs or plant shutdowns. Beyond insuring an adequate level of aggregate demand, perhaps the most important way that the government can facilitate adjustment to the adoption of new techniques is by promoting the necessary adaptability of the labor force through education and training. In this connection, as well as many others, the problems of some of our nation's school systems are noteworthy.

Firms, as well as workers, will have to adjust to technological change, and this too will sometimes be difficult and painful. In recent years, American entrepreneurs and managers have been subjected to considerable criticism. They have been accused of an undue aversion to risk, of paying excessive attention to short-term results to the detriment of the long-term health of their businesses, and of too much reliance on oversimplified analytical tools rather than detailed knowledge and experience with regard to their firms' own productive activities. This is not the place to try to evaluate how much truth there is in these criticisms. But for those firms where some or all of these criticisms are valid, there are likely to be commensurate difficulties in adjusting to the technological changes of the 1980s and 1990s.

Government agencies also face difficult problems in adjusting to technological change. For example, consider the case of the Federal Communications Commission. New technologies have blurred the traditional separation between the regulated communications industry and the unregulated computer industry. The FCC, as well as Congress, must try to insure that federal regulatory policies and procedures take proper account of this fact. In the 1980s and 1990s, government agencies will continually have to adapt their procedures and decisions to take account of emerging new technologies. Unless they do so promptly and effectively, many of the social benefits of these new technologies may be forgone.

Conclusions

The past few years have been a period of reexamination of the American economy. Beset by double-digit inflation, high rates of unemployment, deficits in our balance of trade, basic structural problems in major industries like steel and autos, and very low rates of productivity increase, the American economy, long the engine on which our people (and to some extent other peoples as well) could count for material progress, has seemed to be in trouble. Whether this trouble will prove only temporary depends upon the policies adopted by our government, the actions taken by our firms, and the attitudes of our people. The policies, actions, and attitudes required to revitalize the American economy are of many types. Proper monetary and fiscal policies are essential. And so, among many other things, is proper attention by firms to long-range objectives and to such apparently mundane matters as quality control.

In reacting to current problems, it is very important that policy makers, both in the public and private sectors, recognize the central role played by technology. As pointed out above, 40 percent or more of the long-term increase in output per person employed in the United States has been estimated to be due to technological change. Many measures have been proposed in Washington and elsewhere to reverse the apparent slowdown in the rate of innovation. Some proposals seem to view technology as largely exogenous to the economic system. Until only a few decades ago, economists themselves tended to view it this way, but they no longer do so. Particularly under recent and current conditions, such a view could result in very serious mistakes. In my judgment, one of the most important things to stress is that this view is fundamentally incorrect. On the contrary, as emphasized above, the U.S. rate of innovation is heavily dependent on the general economic climate in the United States (which reflects regulatory and antitrust policies as well as general macroeconomic policy).

Needless to say, this does not mean that many steps to encourage and support civilian technology directly would not be worthwhile. Although relatively little is known about the effects of many of these proposed measures, it seems likely that some of them are worth trying, subject to the general guidelines discussed above. Rather, the point is that unless the United States does a much better job of encouraging investment and economic growth while at the same time restoring price stability, it seems unlikely that direct measures specifically designed to encourage and support civilian technology will have as much effect as is commonly expected.

C. 'Fred Bergsten

7

The International Dimension

The basic goals of U.S. economic policy over the medium and longer terms are to maintain a substantial rate of real economic growth and avoid excessive inflation. It is unclear whether these goals can now be achieved simultaneously by *any* set of purely national policies. Meaningful international coordination of macroeconomic efforts, at least among the major industrial countries, may become imperative for all of them if there is to be satisfactory economic performance for any of them. For the United States, such a reorientation of policy would require a sea change in both intellectual constructs and institutional arrangements—akin to the shift of a generation ago in security thinking and institutions, from "Fortress America" to global alliances in response to the sea change in the nature of the threat to U.S. security and world peace.

C. FRED BERGSTEN *is director of the Institute for International Economics. Dr. Bergsten was formerly assistant secretary for international affairs at the U.S. Department of the Treasury and assistant for international economic affairs to the National Security Council. He has been a senior fellow at the Brookings Institution, Carnegie Endowment for International Peace, and Council on Foreign Relations. He has published twelve books and numerous articles and monographs on a wide range of international economic issues; his most recent is* Trade Policy in the 1980s.

For all the talk of interdependence, virtually all major American macroeconomists continue to employ essentially closed-economy models which treat the external sector as a minor residual. Administrations of both parties have traditionally set U.S. fiscal and other economic policies with little regard to the rest of the world; the Reagan administration has ignored outside factors more thoroughly than its predecessors, but the difference is primarily of degree. The Federal Reserve Board has been more sensitive to international considerations, but to an extensive degree only when the dollar has come under pressure in the foreign exchange markets or external forces otherwise provided an excuse to do what the board wanted to do for domestic reasons anyway.

On this view, much of the focus on improving American competitiveness produces a quite misleading impression. It is certainly imperative to improve American competitiveness—or at least maintain it since, on some indicators, U.S. international competitiveness is in excellent shape. For example, from 1978 to 1980, the volume of U.S. nonagricultural exports grew twice as fast as world trade. In early 1981, the U.S. share of world exports of manufactured goods was higher than it had been since 1970—reversing all losses of competitiveness which had occurred in the earlier 1970s. From early 1978 through early 1981, the U.S. current account improved by about $35 billion (annual rate) despite a rise of over $30 billion in the cost of oil imports. The erosion in the U.S. position since early 1981 is almost wholly due to the severe overvaluation of the dollar in the exchange markets, so there is strong reason to believe that the underlying competitive position of the United States in the world economy remains quite strong.

The implication of much of the current debate, however, is that a successful "restoration of American competitiveness" could enable America to restore substantially more rapid economic progress regardless of the path of the world economy in general. This chapter raises doubts as to whether such an outcome is possible. To do so, it will first analyze the contemporary meaning of international economic interdependence and then turn to the implications for the United States of its deepening dependence on the world economy.

Economic Interdependence in the 1980s

The key empirical fact which emerges from recent economic history is that no major country can alone achieve rapid, sustained economic growth in a slowly growing (or stagnant) world economy. For example:

1. Italy, France, and the United Kingdom all tried to expand their way out of the first oil shock but were hit by currency crises in late 1975 or 1976.
2. The United States, the largest (and presumably most independent) country in the world, tried in 1977–78 but after a modest recovery soon confronted a cumulative run on the dollar and had to reorient its policies toward fighting inflation.
3. France tried under the new Mitterrand government in early 1981 but failed almost totally, checkmated by the external consequences of its plans.
4. Even Japan, the paragon of the industrial nations, has experienced flat growth for about a year despite the lowest interest rates by far among major nations.
5. Korea and Brazil, who were the two fastest growers in the world during 1960–79 and did prove able to ride out the global recession of 1975 by borrowing heavily abroad, experienced deep recessions in 1980 and 1981, respectively, and have been unable to restore their earlier paces.
6. Mexico, the fastest grower in the late 1970s, must now accept very low or even negative growth for an extended period.
7. The other oil exporters, even in the Arabian Gulf, have cut back sharply in the face of the "reverse oil shock" as their volumes and prices have retreated in response to global stagnation.

The similarity among these results seems to derive from similar causes. Productivity has slowed substantially in all of the industrial countries since 1973—more in Japan and several European countries than in the United States. Inflation has risen sharply almost everywhere, constraining the stimulus which can be applied through domestic macroeconomic tools. Sizable budget deficits in many countries have generated widespread concern, further restraining fiscal policy from playing its traditional Keynesian role. Real interest rates have soared. Earlier sources of rapid growth, such as the movement of workers from farm to factory in Europe and Japan, have run their course. Key macroeconomic variables in Europe, such as savings and unemployment rates, have approached American levels as the European economies have reached the U.S. level of per capita income and distribution of labor among the several sectors.

Perhaps most notably, currency declines have choked off expansionary efforts in virtually every country which has tried to break out of the global stagnation on its own. The dollar crisis of 1978 reined in the last U.S. effort to expand aggressively, and the U.S. economy has been essentially flat since 1979. The French franc had to be devalued twice within the first year of the Socialist government. Japan has been pushing interest rates upward since early 1982, despite its own anemic performance and effort to reduce the budget deficit, in an effort to stem the massive depreciation of the yen. Germany sharply tightened its monetary policy in early 1981, because of pressure on the Deutsche mark, despite the contrary needs of the domestic economy. The lesson has been even more obvious in a long list of countries ranging from Belgium through Poland (the Communist countries are hardly immune) and Mexico: he who tries to go it alone, with rapid growth, is slapped down by the markets sooner or later—mostly sooner. In the case of countries with large external borrowing needs, the external constraint has often taken the form of a sharp reduction in the availability of foreign loans.

The steady acceleration of global economic interdependence may thus have brought the world to a point where we have to conceive economic policy in a global rather than national context. Indeed, both the structural slowdown of the last decade and the cyclical slump which has been superimposed on it over the past couple of years appear to be global in nature. Alexander Swoboda, in a paper presented to the International Monetary Fund–National Board of Economic Research Seminar on Policy Interdependence in August 1982, showed that the standard deviation of the six major industrial countries around the mean of their growth rates dropped sharply in the 1974 to 1982 period from the 1960 to 1971 period, and that the degree of association among the other variables tested (inflation rates, money growth rates, interest rate changes) also rose from the first to the second period—"lending some support to the notion of a world business cycle."

Flexible exchange rates have failed to deliver the promised independence for national policies; indeed, globalization of the economic cycle seems to have accelerated under flexible exchange rates from where it was under fixed rates with the alteration in the exchange rate regime changing at most the transmission mechanism across countries. The healthy, stabilizing contracyclicality of the European and North American economies in the 1960s—which may have been possible, or at least facilitated, by the substantially lesser degree of economic interdependence which existed at that time—has disappeared. The steady supergrowth of Japan and the advanced developing countries (ADCs), which seemed largely oblivious to the state of the world economy through the 1960s and well into the 1970s, may have come to an end. Countries have much less "real" than "nominal" sovereignty over the courses of their economies and their economic policies.

There are several reinforcing transmission mechanisms which appear responsible for this globalization of the business cycle:

1. International trade (in both goods and services) itself, due to the sharp increase in the trade-GNP ratio for virtually every country—This ratio virtually doubled for the Organization for Economic Cooperation and Development (OECD) countries as a whole from 1970 to 1980. The near-stagnation of world trade for the 1979 to 1982 period is thus both cause and effect of the pervasive national slowdowns.
2. Exchange rates—In almost all cases, faster growth produces a weaker trade balance which leads to a weaker currency and added inflationary pressures which intensify monetary restraint and choke off the faster growth.
3. International lending—The same progression of events leads to a cutback in the lending which, in many cases, financed the above-average growth in the first place.

In theory, there is one national escape from the global stagnation trap: export-led growth from an initial position of substantial capacity underutilization, obviating both the external (trade deficit) and internal (inflation) constraints. But the feasibility of such an escape probably varies inversely with the share of the particular country in world trade. For a large country facing weak markets abroad, terms-of-trade losses will offset much of the export volume gains even if real prices can be reduced—and the relatively closed nature of most such economies means they would not get much overall economic boost from modest export expansion in any event.

A very small country may be able to make it alone, either "legitimately" (e.g., Singapore; but even its still positive growth rate has been cut in half by the current world slump) or via competitive devaluation (e.g., Sweden in late 1982). However, its very smallness obviates any substantial effect on the world economy and thus does little for the system or the bigger countries. By definition, of course, this escape hatch is not available to very many countries at any one time since in a world of low or zero growth, the shifts in all countries' trade performance taken together produce a roughly zero-sum outcome. This represents an extreme paradox, because large countries have traditionally been viewed as much more independent than small countries, whereas the opposite seems to prevail in today's interdependent world.

In theory, the United States also has a unique escape hatch via the international role of the dollar and its resulting ability to "borrow automatically" to finance external deficits. As observed in 1977–78, however, this is a double-edged sword: diversification from the dollar overhang can *compound* the pressure of a deterioration in the underlying U.S. situation and intensify the need for retrenchment. This prospect is even greater now than in 1977–78, due to the further evolution of the multiple reserve currency system. Philip A. Klein in *Business Cycles in the Postwar Period,* on the basis of simple statistical tests, has reached the heterodox conclusion that the United States has *traditionally* been affected more by cyclical changes in other countries than it has affected others through its own cyclical alterations.

There is probably also a threshold effect. A simple regression by William Cline in *Trade Policy in the 1980s* shows that the volume of OECD imports tends to rise three times as fast as OECD product when the growth of the latter exceeds 1.5 percent annually, but falls three times as fast when OECD growth falls to a slower pace. Trade can thus grow reasonably rapidly even with the world economy advancing at only 1.5 to 2 percent a year. When growth drops to less than 1 percent, however, the cumulative effect on the external sector is quite negative—setting up a downward spiral of the type observed in the early 1930s and again in the recent past.

A specific aspect of increased trade interdependence is the sharp increase in global swings in commodity prices. Virtually all commodity markets, of which oil is only the most notable, are now world-wide in scope. The sharp response of their prices to modest changes in volume produces booms and busts which intensify each swing (and simultaneously sows the seeds of trouble for the next swing, for example, when weak prices discourage the investments needed to produce adequate supplies for the next upswing.) This cycle, in turn, intensifies the amplitude of swings in the global economic cycle.

In sum, there is strong reason to believe that we have entered an era of globalization, or at least widespread internationalization, of the economic cycle in which no single nation can long prevail with objectives or policies which are far out of step with the rest of the world. This may be a new policy setting, at least in degree, for Japan, Germany, France, and even Brazil and Mexico. It would certainly be new for America—as was the need to ally systematically and permanently with Europe, Japan, and others to preserve world peace over the past thirty or forty years.

American Dependence on the World Economy

The role of America will thus be crucial, as it was in the security sphere, in determining whether the need to internationalize economic policy is recognized and acted upon. Indeed, the United States would probably have to take the lead in promoting an internationalization of economic policy making both because its participation would be of decisive importance and because its willingness to enter into such a system would be doubted until demonstrated.

Both structurally and at the margin, America has in fact become deeply dependent on the world economy. At the level of structure: (1) over 20 percent of U.S. industrial output is now exported; (2) two of every five acres of U.S. farmland produce for export; (3) exports provide one of every six jobs in the U.S. manufacturing sector; (4) between 25 and 33 percent of the profits of American firms derive from their international activities, including both trade and investment; (5) the share of trade in U.S. GNP has more than doubled in the last decade; and (6) imports provide more than 50 percent of our needs for twenty-four of the forty-two most critical primary products, most notably oil but including a wide range of strategic as well as economically important raw materials. Even U.S. financial markets, which are usually viewed as dominating world interest rate patterns, now appear to be substantially influenced by foreign developments. David G. Hartman, in an NBER working paper, concludes that 18 to 64 percent of the variation in U.S. commercial paper rates during 1975–78 were due to foreign sources—a phenomenon which he did not find at all in the early 1970s.

Even more impressive than these structural factors are the effects of external events on U.S. economic performance at the margin. For example, the substantial overvaluation of the dollar that developed in 1981–82 has a major impact on the mix of unemployment and inflation; studies at the Federal Reserve Bank of New York indicate that the 20 percent rise in the dollar from mid–1980 to early 1982 will directly reduce the level of GNP by one to one-and-a-half percentage points and cut the level of prices by three to four percentage points by the end of 1983. The dollar appreciation by late 1982 had reached 25 to 30 percent, generating correspondingly greater effects on GNP and inflation.

Similar events, in the opposite direction, have occurred in the recent past. The dollar depreciation of 1977–78 boosted U.S. inflation by about one-and-a-half percentage points. At the same time, restoration of an equilibrium exchange rate for the dollar restored U.S. price competitiveness in world trade and spurred the export boom of 1978–80, cited above, which increased GNP by about as much, in percentage terms, as the current appreciation has cut it.

Another, perhaps more meaningful, way to view this issue is to note the share of total change in the key U.S. economic variables which derives from external events. The expansion in real net exports of goods and services in 1978–80, for example, accounted for 75 percent of the total growth in real U.S. GNP during that period. From the first quarter of 1981 through the third quarter of 1982, about 75 percent of the decline in real GNP arose from

the decline in net exports—the greatest single factor in bringing
on the recession, much larger than the impact of either the housing
slump or the decline in personal consumption (see Table 1). Hence

TABLE 1.   FOREIGN TRADE AND THE U.S. ECONOMY

(In Billions of 1972 Dollars)

	1978	1979	1980	1981	1981 1st Qtr.*	1982 3rd Qtr.*
GNP	1,438.6	1,479.4	1,474.0	1,502.6	1,507.8	1,478.4
Net exports of goods and services	24.0	37.2	50.6	42.0	48.2	25.7
Memo: residential fixed investment (housing)	62.4	59.1	47.2	44.9	49.6	40.7
Memo: personal consumption expenditures on durable goods	146.3	146.6	137.1	140.0	145.3	136.5

* Seasonally adjusted at annual rate.

Source: U.S. Department of Commerce, Bureau of Economic Analysis.

it seems clear that external factors have a major impact on the
U.S. economy, both structurally and at the margin.

Policy recognition of this phenomenon, however, has been
episodic at best. In 1959, the tightness of the final Eisenhower
budget has been attributed by some to concern about the gold
losses of 1958. The policy mix of the Kennedy administration,
combining fiscal stimulus with tight monetary policy, may have
been motivated modestly by continuing concerns about the dollar.
In the summer of 1968, the sterling and gold crises of the previous
months may have enabled the Johnson administration and Chairman Wilbur Mills of the House Ways and Means Committee to
win congressional support for the income tax surcharge, the first
serious effort to check the outbreak of inflation associated with
the Vietnam War. In late 1978, the steady fall of the dollar
forced the Carter administration to reorient its policies toward

fighting inflation and, a year later, the Federal Reserve to alter sharply its methods for attempting to do so as well. All of these were (real or perceived) crisis responses, however, coming along about once per decade. There has been no systematic effort to integrate international considerations into U.S. macroeconomic policy, with the partial exception of the Carter years as described below.

The issue raised in this chapter is whether the United States can henceforth hope to implement successful macroeconomic policies on a purely national basis. If the rest of the world is stagnant, can U.S. growth and employment attain acceptable levels? At a minimum, advocates of a "purely national" approach should be forced to answer this question—perhaps by advocating a slowdown, or even a reversal, of the growth of interdependence via capital controls or other measures. Much more likely, these developments suggest the need for active internationalization of macroeconomic policy.

Internationalizing Economic Policy: Possible Approaches

A number of proposals have been made over the years for internationalizing economic policy, including for the United States. Most of these focus on monetary policy, implicitly leaving fiscal affairs to national authorities. Their ambitiousness ranges from better coordination among existing national monetary authorities through creation of a world central bank to the development of a single national currency for all countries.

"Coordination" of national economic policies, of course, does not require similar policy objectives in all countries. Indeed, the most ambitious effort to coordinate macroeconomic policies so far—the "locomotive" approach of 1977–78, which is discussed more later—explicitly envisaged expansion in some key countries (United States, Germany, Japan) and a continued stabilization focus in others (United Kingdom, Italy, probably France). Despite the increased globalization of the business cycle, countries may be at different points along the cycle, or face different degrees of external constraint, and thus need to adopt differentiated policies.

In addition, there can be a significant difference between *coordinated* policies and *synchronized* policies. In the excessive global boom of 1972–73, for example, there was a synchronized expansion of the major countries with no coordination among them. Indeed, the absence of coordination probably increased the extent of expansionary policy in each country and thus contributed to the subsequent inflationary blowoff. Moreover, a number of countries (including the United States) sought to export their inflation through currency appreciation, unilateral import liberalization, and even export controls—producing an inefficient outcome for individual countries, and certainly for the world as a whole. Conversely, as just noted, one can readily envisage a coordinated international policy configuration which explicitly called for nonsynchronization of the participating countries. (See Table 2 for examples.)

TABLE 2. COORDINATION AND SYNCHRONIZATION OF NATIONAL ECONOMIC POLICIES—ALTERNATIVE COMBINATIONS

	Coordination	*Noncoordination*
Synchronization	Counter global inflation, 1980–1981	Global boom, 1972–1973
Nonsynchronization	"Locomotive" 1977–1978: U.S., Germany, Japan expand; U.K., Italy, France stabilize	U.S. and Europe, 1960s

Better coordination could of course take many forms, and there have already been occasions on which national authorities have moved in concert to alter interest rate levels or respond to undesired exchange rate shifts. The Bank for International Settlements (BIS) provides a forum where the major central banks meet monthly and periodically seek to act together on a particular issue. In practice, however, no systematic collaboration has ever developed on monetary policy—even among the relatively closely knit group of countries making up the European Community (EC), even since they have organized the European Monetary System (EMS).

An early proposal by Charles P. Kindleberger to improve monetary coordination was to add European and Japanese members to the U.S. Federal Open Market Committee. Such a step would explicitly recognize the global primacy of U.S. monetary policy. At the same time, it would recognize the concomitant responsibility of the United States to take full account of the impact of its actions on other countries. In essence, this approach would seek to internationalize U.S. monetary policy—a step which would have been most welcome to countries faced by the enormous pull of high real U.S. interest rates during 1981–82. A more contemporary version of the idea, reflecting the decline in dollar hegemony and the rising international role of other key currencies, might be more reciprocal by having U.S. officials sit in on decision-making meetings of, for example, the Bundesbank and Bank of Japan, as well as vice-versa. One could also imagine an analogue for fiscal policy, via which non-Americans participated in deliberations of the Council of Economic Advisers or even the Troika (comprising the Secretary of Treasury, Director of the Office of Management and Budget, and Chairman of the Council of Economic Advisers) and vice-versa.

A more ambitious proposal, suggested by Ronald I. McKinnon in the June 1982 *American Economic Review,* would seek to create international management of world monetary policy, joining at least Germany and Japan with the United States. It is based on the view that purely national efforts to manage monetary policy, even in the major countries, are doomed to failure by international substitution among the major currencies—notably the Deutsche mark and yen, along with the dollar.

From this perspective, for example, U.S. monetary policy has been much tighter in the recent past than revealed by purely U.S. monetary data—because heavy foreign demand for dollars has sharply increased the need for dollars world-wide and limited the real growth of available liquidity within the United States itself, with no corresponding increase in the supply of dollars from the U.S. monetary authorities. In addition, intervention by the major foreign central banks to avoid further depreciation of their currencies tightened the supply of Deutsche mark and yen and thus contributed to global contraction. Similarly, the rapid price inflation of the early and late 1970s can be explained much better by cumulating the growth of monetary aggregates in these three key currencies than by looking at the relationship between money growth and inflation in any of the countries individually—largely because the reduced international demand for dollars was not matched by any reduction in supplies thereof.

On this view, the three key currency countries should set a joint target for the growth of their three money supplies. When Deutsche mark were being converted into dollars, for example, Germany would correspondingly tighten its monetary policy (to offset the added supply of Deutsche mark), and the United States would ease its monetary policy to accommodate the added demand for dollars. The net effect would be sharply different, it is argued, from the current situation where Germany may well tighten anyway (to defend the Deutsche mark) but the United States will not loosen because it ignores changes in external conditions in implementing its own policy ("passive sterilization"). In terms of our earlier discussion, this would be an example of coordinated policy nonsynchronization.

Either adding non-Americans to the Federal Reserve Board or linking the monetary policies of the United States, Germany, and Japan would represent a quantum leap in internationalizing monetary policy. However, either alternative would continue to rely on national monetary authorities, albeit working much more closely together. Some observers believe that better coordination, even to this extent, would not be enough. Thus they have proposed more ambitious approaches, based on creating new supranational mechanisms to manage monetary policy on a global basis.

A number of these proposals center on creating an international central bank and/or a completely new international money. The earliest postwar versions of this approach envisaged converting the International Monetary Fund into a world central bank, operating throughout the world as needed via open market operations like a national monetary authority. It could buy national government securities when stimulus was needed, and sell them to contract world economic activity. The objective was to assure adequate liquidity for the international financial system in place of the gold-dollar system which was correctly seen as providing an unstable basis for the world economy.

One practical result of these proposals was the creation a decade later of Special Drawing Rights (SDR) at the IMF. SDR are a truly international money, created by an international organization and without tangible "backing." Their original objective was to become the world's "primary reserve asset," and various schemes over the years have seen them as the *sole* monetary instrument for international use among central banks. In addition, consideration has been given to the use of SDR in the private sector, and there has been some growth in interest in them as a unit of account in recent years.

Several experienced observers have also called for creating a world central bank. They have done so primarily because of the growing interdependence of the world economy, as outlined in the previous section of this paper. All such proposals would build on the existing IMF, providing for it, of course, an enormous increase in authority and policy instruments.

The most ambitious of the policy internationalization ideas explicitly envisages creation of a global currency, to be used throughout the world for all private and official transactions. In essence, this would permit replication on a global scale of national monetary policy within a completely closed economy. Such a world would approximate a system of unalterably fixed exchange rates, with international capital flows having affects akin to interregional flows within nations. Under some versions of this approach, fiscal policy would remain national and would be assigned the task of coping with adjustment to the macroeconomic changes required by overall global considerations.

No attempt is made here to assess these proposals, which are presented primarily to indicate that the need to internationalize economic (especially monetary) policy has been recognized for many years by some observers, both theoreticians and practitioners, and that ideas exist for how to do so. Any such approach would obviously have to be developed in much greater detail than has been done to date, of course, with a particular eye to political and institutional considerations in the United States and other countries. Nevertheless, numerous schemes exist and could provide a basis for practical proposals when and if there was a desire to seek such an approach.

Internationalizing Economic Policy: Experience to Date

There have already been embryonic efforts to internationalize economic policy. Indeed, fostering improvement in the coordination of national economic policies is a major task of several international organizations, notably the OECD and IMF. The currency of the topic is indicated by the creation at the Versailles Summit in June 1982 of yet another group, this time among the "Big Five" (U.S., Germany, Japan, France, U.K.) along with IMF management, to enhance their surveillance of world economic developments.

In practice, two attempts at international policy coordination deserve particular mention. One is the ongoing effort of the EC, over its first twenty-five years of existence, to forge a greater coordination of macroeconomic policy among its member countries. In recent years, this took the form of creating the EMS—whose second stage envisaged extensive supranational decision making by a European Monetary Fund.

To date, the EC effort has doubtlessly produced more policy coordination than would have occurred in the absence thereof—and less extreme exchange rate movements than have occurred for nonmember currencies (notably the dollar, yen, and pound). At the same time, that effort has been disappointing in terms of fostering significantly closer linking of policy formulation in its major countries. In part, this is because both chosen vehicles for the effort—the "snake" approach of the early 1970s and the EMS of the late 1970s—sought to induce close policy links indirectly by maintaining fixed parities within specified margins among the member countries, rather than by setting up mechanisms for direct policy coordination. In practice, the countries have continued to experience substantial divergences in growth and inflation rates, and have chosen to change their exchange rates periodically rather than bring their national economic policies into closer accord. On the whole, the European experience is not terribly encouraging in terms of effective policy internationalization.

The second relevant experience was the effort by the Carter administration, upon taking office in 1977, to advance what came to be known as the "locomotive" approach. As of late 1976, only the United States was recovering with any vigor from the world recession of 1975. The new administration took the view that U.S. recovery alone would be inadequate to promote acceptable levels of world growth, which was of crucial importance politically as well as economically because of the threat of Communist participation in a number of European governments and the growing plight of the developing countries. Moreover, they feared—correctly, as it turned out—that the U.S. recovery would abort if not joined by others, because of the inevitable deterioration in the U.S. external accounts and the position of the dollar.

From the outset of the administration, therefore, Carter officials pushed hard for stimulus policies in the several key countries where inflation was seemingly under control and external surpluses, if increased further, threatened to cause international monetary instability: primarily Germany and Japan, and, to a lesser extent, Switzerland and the Netherlands. The other major countries—especially the U.K. and Italy, but also France—still faced severe inflation and balance of payments problems, and thus were counseled to remain committed to stabilization programs.

Throughout 1977, Germany and Japan resisted the proposals, and the consequences expected by the Carter officials began to eventuate. However, at the Bonn Summit in mid-1978, both Germany and Japan, along with France, committed themselves to adopt expansionary macroeconomic policies and fulfilled their pledges later in the year. Interestingly, these efforts were implemented almost wholly by changes in fiscal policy—in contrast to the focus on monetary coordination in most of the scholarly work on the issue.

By the time these steps were taken, however, a full-blown dollar crisis had hit the United States and forced a reorientation of its policies toward fighting inflation. The German and Japanese expansions thus came a year or so late and are widely viewed as having contributed to the sharp increase in inflation and record current account deficits which subsequently hit both countries —though the GNP deflator did not rise in either country in 1979, and the second oil shock was surely more critical in causing their later problems. In any event, the failure to coordinate effectively contributed to a sequence of economic and monetary instability in the major economies and currencies rather than the synchronized expansion which was sought—and might have occurred had the United States waited for the others to launch its own expansion program, or had the others joined the United States in early 1977 rather than late 1978. Indeed, there remain negative memories of this episode at least in Germany—though the adverse effects came as much or more from the *delay* in implementing the coordinated strategy as from its substantive impact.

Since the reemergence of double-digit price increases in the late 1970s, national economic policies in most of the major countries have aimed at fighting inflation. In practice, however, there has been very little coordination of these efforts, although the basic approach has been encouraged by each subsequent international meeting of high officials, most recently the Versailles Summit and the annual meeting of the IMF at Toronto in September 1982. Partly as a result, the world has now been plunged into a deep slump with a downward spiral of world trade, huge monetary imbalances, and cumulating debt crises. The current situation, on the downside, is parallel to the uncoordinated global boom of 1972–73 which helped produce the initial burst of double-digit inflation and perhaps the first oil shock.

Conclusion

Barring an extensive retreat into protectionism or segmentation of the international capital market by direct controls or interest equalization taxes, the internationalization of the U.S. economy is likely to continue to grow throughout this decade and beyond. Hence it will become increasingly difficult to envisage the implementation of effective macroeconomic policies on the purely national level. The United States may retain nominal sovereignty over its economic policy, but the degree of real control which it can exercise in practice is much more limited.

At a minimum, it seems likely that efforts will be needed to coordinate U.S. policy with that of the other major industrialized countries, notably Germany and Japan, but also the rest of the EC and Canada. On some issues, such as debt and trade, key developing countries will need to be involved as well.

To some extent, existing institutional arrangements can be used to accomplish the needed coordination. Particularly for monetary policy, however, new groupings of countries and modalities of coordination will probably have to emerge. Much of the effort will be informal and limited to the key countries at first, as in all effective international coordination, with more formal ratification in the institutions with larger memberships coming at a later stage. An initial step might be to invite representatives of the Bundesbank and Bank of Japan to participate as observers at meetings of the Federal Reserve Board and Federal Open Market Committee, with Federal Reserve officials likewise attending policy-making sessions of the Bundesbank and Bank of Japan.

For the purposes of this volume, however, the key point is not the details or the vehicles but the concept. A serious U.S. decision to begin to internationalize its economic policy would represent a dramatic change of significance comparable to the U.S. decision immediately after World War II to begin to internationalize its security policy. In both cases, an essential element is the active cooperation of other major countries—some of which might well resist economic policy coordination for a time, just as some resisted security coordination for quite a while. But other countries are ultimately likely to be receptive to both ideas, because of their greater vulnerability to outside forces and inability to go it alone. U.S. leadership, both intellectual and political, is the crucial ingredient to launch this entire approach—and needs to be made a part of any comprehensive U.S. economic strategy for the remainder of this decade and beyond.

Index

Absenteeism, 121
Aggregative policies, 17, 19
Agriculture, 107
   price shocks, 88
   recombinant DNA technology and, 129
   trade, 41
Aid to Families with Dependent Children (AFDC), 67, 116-17
Alaskan natural gas pipeline, 49
American Association for the Advancement of Science, 130
Antitrust laws, 30, 47, 50
Automation, 106-9, 131
Automobile industry, 47-48, 108
Ayres, Robert V., 108

Balanced federal budget, 7-8, 23-24
Balance of trade, 142
Bank for International Settlement (BIS), 161
Bank reserves, 10, 73, 95-99
Bankruptcy, 78
Bendick, Marc, 118
Bergsten, C. Fred, 151-68
Biotechnology, 128-30
Block grants, 66
Blue-collar occupations, 107
Bonn Summit (1978), 166
Bonuses, 122
Bracket creep, 19, 54
Brain drain, 38
Braniff International, 42
Brazil, 153
Buchanan, James M., 65-66
Budget (see Fiscal management)
Bureau of Labor Statistics (BLS), 106, 115, 132
Business capital formation, 76-79
Business cycle, 17, 24, 55, 96
   globalization of, 155, 160

CAD/CAM automated factory, 131
Canada, 145
Capital formation, 2, 76-79
Carter administration, 51, 159, 169, 165-67
CETA (Comprehensive Employment and Training Act), 110, 116
Chemical industries, 134, 135, 146
Chrysler Corporation, 42, 49
Citibank, 121
Cline, William, 156
College education, 115, 123
Commodity prices, 157
Competition, 30-32, 37-38, 152
   education and training and, 45-46
   institutional changes and, 47-51
   need for, 40-41
Computer-assisted instruction, 114
Computer-based technologies, 106
Congressional Budget Office, 60
Congressional budget process, 59-61, 67, 82-83
Congressional investment banking, 49
Constitution of the United States, 64-65, 82
Consumption orientation, 28-30
Continental Airlines, 42
Corporate income taxes, 9
Council of Economic Advisers, 132
Credit, 4, 9, 22, 28
   total net, 91-92, 98
Cummins Engine Corporation, 121

Defense spending, 4, 25, 53-55, 57, 68, 69
Democracy, 20, 21, 27
Denison, Edward, 128
Deposit interest ceilings, 86
Devine, Judith R., 118
Disability insurance, 103
Disadvantaged, training for, 115-18, 124

About The American Assembly

The American Assembly was established by Dwight D. Eisenhower at Columbia University in 1950. It holds nonpartisan meetings and publishes authoritative books to illuminate issues of United States policy.

An affiliate of Columbia, with offices in the Fairchild Center, the Assembly is a national educational institution incorporated in the State of New York.

The Assembly seeks to provide information, stimulate discussion, and evoke independent conclusions in matters of vital public interest.

AMERICAN ASSEMBLY SESSIONS

At least two national programs are initiated each year. Authorities are retained to write background papers presenting essential data and defining the main issues in each subject.

A group of men and women representing a broad range of experience, competence, and American leadership meet for several days to discuss the Assembly topic and consider alternatives for national policy.

All Assemblies follow the same procedure. The background papers are sent to participants in advance of the Assembly. The Assembly meets in small groups for four or five lengthy periods. All groups use the same agenda. At the close of these informal sessions, participants adopt in plenary session a final report of findings and recommendations.

Regional, state, and local Assemblies are held following the national session at Arden House. Assemblies have also been held in England, Switzerland, Malaysia, Canada, the Caribbean, South America, Central America, the Philippines, and Japan. Over one hundred thirty institutions have cosponsored one or more Assemblies.

ARDEN HOUSE

Home of The American Assembly and scene of the national sessions is Arden House which was given to Columbia University in 1950 by W. Averell Harriman. E. Roland Harriman joined his brother in contributing toward adaptation of the property for conference purposes. The buildings and surrounding land, known as the Harriman Campus of Columbia University, are 50 miles north of New York City.

Arden House is a distinguished conference center. It is self-support-ing and operates throughout the year for use by organizations with educational objectives.

AMERICAN ASSEMBLY BOOKS

The background papers for each Assembly are published in cloth and paperbound editions for use by individuals, libraries, businesses, public agencies, nongovernmental organizations, educational insti-tutions, discussion and service groups. In this way the deliberations of Assembly sessions are continued and extended.

The subjects of Assembly programs to date are:

1951——United States-Western Europe Relationships
1952——Inflation
1953——Economic Security for Americans
1954——The United States' Stake in the United Nations
——The Federal Government Service
1955——United States Agriculture
——The Forty-Eight States
1956——The Representation of the United States Abroad
——The United States and the Far East
1957——International Stability and Progress
——Atoms for Power
1958——The United States and Africa
——United States Monetary Policy
1959——Wages, Prices, Profits, and Productivity
——The United States and Latin America
1960——The Federal Government and Higher Education
——The Secretary of State
——Goals for Americans
1961——Arms Control: Issues for the Public
——Outer Space: Prospects for Man and Society
1962——Automation and Technological Change
——Cultural Affairs and Foreign Relations
1963——The Population Dilemma
——The United States and the Middle East
1964——The United States and Canada
——The Congress and America's Future
1965——The Courts, the Public, and the Law Explosion

1965——The United States and Japan
1966——State Legislatures in American Politics
——A World of Nuclear Powers?
——The United States and the Philippines
——Challenges to Collective Bargaining
1967——The United States and Eastern Europe
——Ombudsmen for American Government?
1968——Uses of the Seas
——Law in a Changing America
——Overcoming World Hunger
1969——Black Economic Development
——The States and the Urban Crisis
1970——The Health of Americans
——The United States and the Caribbean
1971——The Future of American Transportation
——Public Workers and Public Unions
1972——The Future of Foundations
——Prisoners in America
1973——The Worker and the Job
——Choosing the President
1974——The Good Earth of America
——On Understanding Art Museums
——Global Companies
1975——Law and the American Future
——Women and the American Economy
1976——Nuclear Power Controversy
——Jobs for Americans
——Capital for Productivity and Jobs
1977——The Ethics of Corporate Conduct
——The Performing Arts and American Society
1978——Running the American Corporation
——Race for the Presidency
1979——Energy Conservation and Public Policy
——Disorders in Higher Education
——Youth Employment and Public Policy
1980——The Economy and the President
——The Farm and the City
——Mexico and the United States
1981——The China Factor
——Military Service in the United States
——Ethnic Relations in America
1982——The Future of American Political Parties

1982——Regrowing the American Economy
1983——The Future of American Financial Services Institutions

Second Editions, Revised:

1962——The United States and the Far East
1963——The United States and Latin America
——The United States and Africa
1964——United States Monetary Policy
1965——The Federal Government Service
——The Representation of the United States Abroad
1968——Cultural Affairs and Foreign Relations
——Outer Space: Prospects for Man and Society
1969——The Population Dilemma
1973——The Congress and America's Future
1975——The United States and Japan